the chateaux of the loire

collection "life in france"

the chateaux of the loire

Armand
Lanoux

Translated by Mary Ann Hargrove-Schneilin

éditions sun/paris

Photographs

Jacques Fronval
Rosine Mazin
Gérard Sioën
Claude Rives
Bernard and Catherine Desjeux
Jacques Lang
Michel Guillard
Christian Sappa
Léo Pélissier
Patrick Lorne
Roger Morin

Summary

The Loire
is a Novel

by
Armand Lanoux
of the Goncourt Academy

The Loire is a novel in which the châteaux are the scenery, as the water flows and as time flows. To tell this tale of the river, the *Loire Story,* from prehistoric times to the day of concrete-mixers, we must resort to what is commonly known as "sentimental" geography, a term often used without giving credit to its inventors, since historians, like clowns, are pillagers.

I have seen this technique used in masterly fashion by dear friends, all of whom were snooty travellers smitten with topography, gastronomy and anecdotes, and who were above all poets who didn't mind associating with old tellers of tales or frequenting more or less ill-famed inns, bawdyhouses and "dives" in the footsteps of Villon, Ronsard and even Charles of Orleans and young Balzac, on the lookout for a beautiful pair of shoulders. They were Pierre MacOrlan, Alexandre Arnoux and Léon-Paul Fargue, to name only three.

I in turn have applied this technique which consists in putting side by side a wine and a line of poetry, in bringing together gallants and ladies born three centuries apart and in putting to my own use river chanteys and artisans' signs; I have used it for Paris and the garden of France, the Unknown Girl of the Seine and my sister, the Loire. Our way of telling tales was, moreover, not so new as our elders thought. Stendhal, Hugo and Alexandre Dumas excelled at it, not to speak of a too thoroughly forgotten doctrinaire, Taine of the Ardennes, whose name is always preceded by the formal "Mister" reserved to "Mister Bertin" who was painted by "Mister Ingres": Mister Taine.

It is indeed to the philosopher from Vouziers, who bore the fine Christian name of Hippolyte, who was first-prize winner in the *Concours Général* (an academic competition for high school students), first of his class at the *Ecole Normale Supérieure,* supercilious collaborator of the *Revue des Deux Mondes* and the *Journal des Débats,* traveller in the Pyrenees, England, Germany and Italy, the shrewd goateed and pince-nezed professor, that we owe the philosophy that permits us to play this game of bubbles known as sentimental geography and which is subject, in the same way as painting or wine, to the latent forces then called "race, time and environment". For it is indeed this man from the Ardennes who wrote of La Fontaine: "*One can consider man as an animal of a superior species that produces philosophies and poems in about the same way that silkworms make their cocoons and bees their hives.”* There have been silkworms on the banks of the Loire and innumerable bees. It is to this pseudo-pedant (for he had a secret sense of humor) that we are indebted for the sentence that delighted Zola and shocked Napoleon III: *“Vice and virtue are products like vitriol and sugar.”* It is rather piquant to think that the airiest art of writing about landscapes is due to this frenzied determinist, and precisely that concerning the Loire, of which he said with much grace for so homely a man: *“A garden tilled a little haphazardly, with negligence and brilliant discoveries.”*

Hippolyte practised sentimental geography without saying so as his elder, Michelet, had invented sentimental history, which is not the most untrue. Only Malraux was lacking to perfect sentimental art criticism. This was in short the spirit of MacOrlan, Arnoux and Fargue, all survivors of the First World War who had learned through brutal contact with events that, though history and geography require figures and dates, they also need tales.

One last reference before we plunge into this illustrated chronicle of the châteaux of the Loire, their ladies and songs. Giraudoux, the neighbor from Bellac, neighbor of the South, could have added to his repertory of fallacious characters that of Inspector of Forests and Waterways of familiar mythology, who depends directly from the Ministry of the Collective Imagination.

I have met this character, who was invented by Christian Bérard or Malclès. He is a little bit of a prefect, a little bit of a civil engineer, half Robert Houdin, the illusionist and magician from Blois, half Gaudissart, the travelling salesman from Vouvray, who spends his spare time fishing for river shad in the stream (as the Loire is called in Touraine), drawing up the family tree of the Babou de la Bourdaisières (I'll speak again later of this gracious dynasty), laying out between Talcy and the Loire a road of roses that rivals that of Doué-la-Fontaine, and writing the outlines of "sound and light" performances for châteaux submerged by the great equinoctical floods of tourists.

This clerk created by Giraudoux lives in a pleasant *ex officio* apartment on the water's edge at Blois, near France's most beautiful bridge, which is characterized by its airy pyramid in the middle where, between North and South, two tritons bear the coat-of-arms of France, Blois the land of average and extreme reason, domain of the good deputy and mayor Pierre Sudreau. Or he may live in the Golden Isle at Amboise, where a Scottish queen of seven days was brought up; that is, she was only seven days old when she became sovereign, which is a record. She was a princess of the exiled in reverse, for it was her adopted country she longed for and not the one of her birth: Mary Stuart, who so gracefully sang, while she still had her head:

> *Farewell, pleasant land of France*
> *O my homeland*
> *Most dear*
> *Which nurtured my childhood*
> *Farewell, France, farewell, my happy days.*

We all know what followed. To tell the novel of the Loire in the manner of the kingfisher, the symbol of these low, golden banks, we must have near us this exquisitely nearsighted person of distinction. He alone can give some coherence to remarks bandied about by turtle doves from turret to turret, the château being the geometrical place of this median region of the French meadowland that Mary made her own.

II

The château reigns over the Loire. I could easily name three hundred, and there are at least a thousand. The château prevails by far over the basilica, the abbey and the city hall. An underhanded war went on over the centuries between the lord, the bishop and the magistrate: the king's man, God's man and the City's man. The former won.

There was no lack of saints, though, and they were some of the best, with St. Benedict at one end and St. Martin at the other. In spite of their high quality, the Loire remains princely and secular, luxurious, luxuriant and sometimes lecherous, being constant only in frivolity. The song of the world, as the great Lurçat was to say, prevailed over matins. Rabelais, who was curate of Meudon but a son of Chinon, is closer to the abbey of Thélème than to a Trappist monastery. He is more than a little proud of his native Devinière: "For I was born and was early nurtured in the garden of France, which is Touraine." Of course, there have been mishaps. In whimsicality there is as much of divine grace as of the devil. Sister Beatrice was in charge of the turning-box at her convent. One day she laid her keys before the statue of Mary and left. For fifteen years Beatrice led a very shameful life, until one day she met the superintendant of the monastery, who did not recognize her, and she defiantly asked him what had become of Sister Beatrice. "She is doing very well. She is now head of the novices and everyone loves her." Beatrice returned to the convent and asked to see the person who was using her name. When she saw *her* coming, Beatrice fell on her knees. This happened at Fontevrault, long ago.

Yet in the Loire country and especially in what concerns architecture, frivolity carries more weight than solemnity. Tufa, the stone of the Loire, which is the color of Vouvray wine and sparkles with mica, is easy to cut as soon as the air reaches it (a fact appreciated by a population that detests useless labor, as all the popular sayings indicate and Balzac too, who unscrupulously gives credit to his compatriot's reputation for indolence: "As for his laziness, it is sublime and is admirably expressed by this popular saying: 'Man of Touraine, would you like some soup ? Yes. Then bring me your bowl. I'm no longer hungry.' "). This golden stone even has the advantage of hardening when exposed to air, which is the peak of complaisance for a building stone! It is evident that such an agreeable material is better suited to favorites' palaces than to monks' cells.

But what about the burgers, who were not so poor themselves? How is it that they, contrary to their Nordic brothers, let themselves be supplanted? The burgers of Orleans looked sceptically upon Joan of Arc's idealistic ride. In reference to them gentle Maurice Genevoix–and here *gentle* is taken in its medieval sense, which is not insipid–recalls the ancient adage:

Orleans, city of lucre
Carefully keeps its Saint-Frusquin (worldly goods).

(The expression, which is in the spirit of St. Paycheck, St. World-Without-End and St. Farce, is distinctly pejorative.) Were they not tough enough to resist chaplain and duke? They were indeed not able to do so, being betrayed perhaps by the indolence of a river that grows as it slopes down to the sea. Only a few leagues away the burgers of Blois were much more openhanded and so quick to spend their money that the same secular litany had it that:

> *Blois, city of parvenus,*
> *Gaily devours its revenue.*

Their brothers of Tours readily loosen their pursestrings:

> *Tours, city of carnival,*
> *Devours interest and capital.*

And if one continues in the same fashion, one comes to Angers:

> *Low city and high bell-towers,*
> *Rich prostitutes and poor scholars.*

The last two sayings appear to be by François Villon, who also knew his sentimental geography, since he had learned it through his shoe soles. The further one goes toward the mouth of the longest and *most useless* of our rivers (this remark too is by Maurice Genevoix, the language poacher), the more one sees the pleasant life prevail over the frenzy to possess. In short, it is as if, from Orleans to Angers, the river carried with it the last traces of the ruthlessness traditionally said to be characteristic of the harsh Auvergnats of the Upper-Loire, Orleans being situated in the middle, between the avarice of the mountain and the *dolce vita* of the plain.

In imitation of their princes, the burgers of the Loire found other things to do with the money they acquired in trade on the great river than to build proud town halls like their Picard and Flemish brothers. The king and his court were no doubt too near for two centuries, with falcons on their shoulders and cup-and-ball toys in their hands. There are no belfries in the Loire country and just enough monasteries and abbeys. The only things that count are the châteaux, from the private home to Chambord, according to fortune and rank, and from the citadel of Angers, an awesome fortress, to the most recent, the Pompadour's candy box at Ménars, in chronological order. Fort, fortress, castle, château, manor-house, residence, private home, folly, hunting lodge and love nest, this is the whole range of castle life.

"Châteaux in France and not in Spain, for there are châteaux only in France and the Loire of our kings is the sovereign of Touraine", observed Paul Fort, another gentle-man, in his ballad, not out of chauvinism, since he was born at Rheims, but through love of Germaine, his Touraine beauty.

The story should be told in the manner of an overture for flute. I do it all the more gladly that I knew the actors in it. Paul Fort was not yet prince of poets; he wore a Rembrandt hat and a Lavalliere tie, had hollow cheeks and a "long drooping Valois nose", was in short a poet, when he saw again at Sully-on-Loire, at the very gate to the Vale, "a very young girl, discreet, slender, with a flexible waist like Diana the Huntress" whom he had already noticed at the Closerie des Lilas, his fief at Montparnasse before the artists took over.

This time the poet caught fire and the Bordes woodlands resounded with the cries of a post-Symbolist faun and with poetry modulated by the purest tenderness found in any of Fort's verse:

> *"When you lean your face toward me your hair takes the exact shape of the clouds, but I see through its fluttering screen the trembling Loire, the silver-waved Loire."*

Bullseye! Here is the woman Loire on her terrace.

Alas, the Rheims Rembrandt was married! Such things do happen, even to poets. Germaine's father called him an Attila when he heard the news: *"Sir, Attila respected his hosts' daughters. You have behaved like a barbarian. Your soul is viler than that of the king of the Huns!"* The father refused to recognize the fact that the Touraine beauty did not respect the Attila of free verse any more than he himself did! Germaine gave me this poem, of which she is the star, disguised as a château, of course: *"Chambord, Chinon, Loches, Azay, in truth where my loves came alive to love, you must see the Orleanais, my beloved Sully-on-Loire, reflecting her face in the Loire and its mirrors..."*

So Germaine was for Paul the "sweetest of châteaux". We don't need to have recourse to Freud here. All his life Paul Fort loved the Touraine lady (who was really from Orleans, but Touraine sounded better). A half-century went by before he could marry her. It was on St. Medard's Day in 1956. I was there. It was raining as in the song by Brassens, who was also there.

III

There is a well-known anecdote about an Englishman who, while visiting the Loire, wrote in his diary the first day: *"Castles"*. The second: *"Many castles"*. The third: *"Too many castles"*.

The "products" of the Loire civilization are indeed the castle and the château, multiform and innumerable, and any reflection upon the river must include the psychoanalysis of castle and château. Well, the male castle and the female château carry on a dialogue. The male castle is war and pride, the female château is charm and is not always careful in her choice of means.

Which are the male castles? First, there is Angers. Here still reigns the decapitated fortress that could not be humbled by royal punishment. Looking toward the stormy West, with is great mass it gives the lie to the "gentleness of Anjou" praised by Joachim du Bellay in these famous lines:

"More do I love...
... my Gallic Loire than the Latin Tiber
More my little Liré than the Mount Palatine
And more than sea air the gentleness of Anjou."

These *Regrets* still endure, precisely as one looks at the black and grey castle that is their petrified counterpoint.

The Loire did not lack for courtier-poets whom we would call its "public relations men"! The Inspector of Commonplaces, our companion created by Giraudoux, would point out that there is also an Angevin ruthlessness that has been expressed with great vigor during the last few decades by Hervé Bazin, author of *Vipère au poing* and who was reared in Anjou. This ruthlessness was incarnated very long ago by the barbarous Foulques Nerra, the Black Falcon, lord of the locality (who had the same haircut as Foloche's son), holed up with his iron-clad henchmen in his castle at the end of the world.

A chill runs up your spine at the sight of these seventeen round towers clinging to their rocky foundations. This castle bears witness to the harshness of the Nerras, whose first Count was Foulques the Red, who must have been fairly close to a beast. The Foulques, especially Nerra the third, great eaters of Bretons and fierce enemies of the Counts of Blois, left their predatory imprints as far as Chambord.

The Anjou Caesar was a bigotted slaughterer. In 1025 he pillaged Saumur, burned the monasteries and exterminated the subjects of the Count of Blois. Then, having repented, during the Crusades he punished himself by having himself dragged through the streets of Jerusalem and whipped by his valets! He then had the valets whipped in turn because they had not beaten him hard enough! When this brutish Knight Templar returned from the Orient, he found his son master of his county. He defeated him in battle and then made him wear a saddle on his back! "You are broken in at last!" said Foulques. "Yes, but by my father!" said the son. This sounds like a play by Claudel!

One must see this dual aspect of ferocity and langor to understand the Loire. Its tapestry, whose capital is Angers, bears witness to this fact, with, on the one hand, the *Apocalypse Tapestry* and Jean Lurçat's magnificent group, the *Song of the World*, and, on the other hand, in the spirit of du Bellay, the gentleness of the woolen millefiori for all the *Ladies with Unicorn* of courtly love.

The other virile pole, at the other end of the Vale, is Chambord, the "macho" dream of our most paranoid sovereign, Francis I. Although mores have become milder since the days of Foulques Nerra, this castle or château is nonetheless a delirium in stone. Chambord is beautiful and mad, almost as much so as the castles of Ludwig II of Bavaria. This was seen by all the poets, like Vigny, proud singer of the wolf and death (we are here on the outskirts of Sologne), who writes: *"Four leagues from Blois, and one from the Loire, in a very low little valley between muddy marshes and a wood of great oaks, far from all roads, one comes suddenly upon a royal or rather a magic château. One would say that, compelled by some wonderful lamp, a genie of the Orient had carried it off during one of the thousand and one nights, had stolen it away from the land of sunshine and hidden it in the land of fog."*

A model of inspired sentimental geography, it has everything: the singing quality of the prose, the contrast between delirium and landscape and the beauty of the images. The author of *Cinq-Mars,* another novel of the Loire, understood the whimsy of the Prince who got revenge for his humiliation at Pavia through this stony ostentation.

There has been much disagreement as to who built it, Boccador, Denis Sourdeau, Pierre Nepveu or even Leonardo da Vinci. The real architect was Francis I.

Seen in the light of symbolism in the fashion of Bachelard, Chambord is a scenic site beyond comparison for the hunt and the drama. Indeed, this wonder had as its only (costly) object the showing of lords on horseback to squealing skewers of court ladies on the terraces. Thus a village of turrets and blue façades tops a pre-classical building of which Paul Vitry, one of our best art historians, rightly said: *"Love of regularity and solicitude for the colossal are thus exaggerated almost to the absurd... Chambord is one of the first manifestations of the architectural megalomania that leads to Versailles."*

Let's carry things to the absurd point the archeologist speaks of. The classical part always remained deserted while royal weekend parties enlivened the 440 rooms composing this hanging village, with as many chimneys as there are days in the year and as many salamanders as mistresses of the king, his beautiful busty sweethearts coming and going forty meters from the ground. Yes, as much as Palladio's celebrated theater at Vicenza, it is pure, unadulterated theatrical illusion. The double spiral staircase of Chambord where two lovers can go up and down without ever meeting, is the machinery of a permanent show. The lavish Francis was nonetheless its first victim, as Brantôme told: *"Of all the women I ever saw with him and knew him to have,*

18

I never saw one who did not go more eagerly with him than his pack of hounds after the deer." It is true that Brantôme was a misogynist. King Francis nonetheless engraved one day on a window pane in his study after experiencing a disappointment, the famous saying: *"Woman often varies, the man who trusts her is a fool"* At least it was told this way. Brantôme is briefer. The king just scratched these definitive words: *"Every woman varies."*

Louis XIV, the Sun King, after the Salamander King, came by chance to Chambord, which under his reign was no longer "in" (he came here nine times in all), broke the insolent pane at the request of a pretty, lame woman, another Touraine beauty, Louise de la Baume Le Blanc, to whom he gave the estate of La Vallière. Louis was unfaithful because Louise was too wellbehaved. She reproached him for it tenderly and became a Carmelite.

IV

And the other castles of Adam? There *are* others, like Langeais, still a fortress, though built rather late, around 1465, a bewitching structure where the machicolations threaten and the postern frowns; Chinon, set in its forest, where the shade of Joan of Arc recognizing Charles VII alternates with that of turgescent Rabelais telling the adventures of Panurge, not to speak of those of the Knights Templar, Chinon, founded by Cain; Loches, austere in spite of Agnes Sorel, mistress of Charles VII, a castle famous for its prisons; Montsoreau, celebrated in the cloak and dagger tales of Alexandre Dumas; Beaugency and Meung, where François Villon moped, and many others!

And Eve's castles? I know of as many, particularly Chenonceau, Azay-le-Ridel and Ussé.

Chenonceau is, inversely, as typical as Chambord. There are reasons for this. It was the favorite residence of the divine Diane of Poitiers, the greatest of the *éminences roses* who reigned vicariously through kings. First, architecturally Chenonceau is a feminine counterpoint to Chambord and one of equal absurdity. On a day when the sky is not entirely blue (a prerequisite if one is to fully savor the Loire sky), but is whimsical, when a few contorted clouds come from the ocean, the contrast between the masonry, which is of a rouged pallor (the adjective corresponds to the basic color of tufa), and the starched roofs, becomes exquisite. In these repeated arches there is a rhythm that reminds one of womanly charms, even to the indolent straddling of the Cher (and the author wonders if he has not written something indecent).

The unity of inspiration is due to the fact that only women have lived at Chenonceau. Francis I, like all kings, had financiers. One was named Thomas Bohier. It was for his wife, Catherine, that Bohier had the château built around 1515 (memorable year)! The château passed next to Diane of Poitiers, the supposed favorite of Francis I and the uncontested favorite of Henry II, although the young king was twenty years younger than she. But Francis's son already had a wife, Catherine de' Medici, whose jealousy was all the more justified as her royal husband had only one mistress, and this, as any woman will confirm, aggravated the situation. Catherine was well aware of her misfortune. She had seen Diane with her own eyes! Brantôme tells us how Catherine had had a hole bored *above the bedroom of the aforesaid lady, in order to see everything and the life they led together.* The queen was properly punished for her curiosity because she and her chambermaid, who was her accomplice, *saw nothing but what was very handsome, for they perceived a woman who was very beautiful, white, delicate and very fresh, half in a nightgown and half naked, caress her lover, treat him with delicacy and romp about with him and her lover do the same with her...*

Everyone knows what followed. Henry II died of an on-the-job accident (a fatal lance thrust given by an opponent in a tournament in 1559). Catherine, who was widow and regent, did not fail to take her revenge. The court expected this episode. Catherine de' Medici also owned Chaumont castle. Chaumont is not a charming château. Built on a rock as it is, with heavy towers, machicolations, bartizans and an immense drawbridge, it lacks only Victor Hugo to paint it in black-wash. In the documentation room is the portrait of a beautiful person with a small, fleshy, slightly pouting mouth, a sensual nose, and a round forehead above eyes sparkling with mischief. A crescent moon tells us who she is. She is indeed Diane. Diane as the goddess Diana.

What is she doing here, this creature who is still magnificent at the age of sixty? Well, she is bored. She still does not understand what has happened to her. Indeed, the all-powerful Florentine obtained her revenge only by forcing Diane to exchange gay Chenonceau for gloomy Chaumont. The regent and mother of the new king, the small Francis II, took no other measures against her rival, whom she crudely called "Old Lady Poitiers". The preceding year still, a correspondant of the duke of Ferrara spelled out in detail to his master Catherine's crude remark concerning Diane: "In this kingdom, there are too many whores running the king's business!"

So why this mildness? For reasons of State? They were both fierce partisans of the Catholic faction. But what else? The records suggest that there existed between the two women a "gentlewomen's agreement". Catherine had feared repudiation. In spite of the difference in age, she was unable to compete with "the Poitiers woman" in the king's heart. The ambassador Giacomo Cappello said politely of her: "She is a beautiful woman when her face is veiled."

And too, Catherine had organized an escort of "bewitchers" whom she charged with very special missions; this was her "flying squadron". That gives some weight to the idea that the beautiful old woman and the ugly young one had arranged between them that the king would not be unfaithful to them.

The Medici woman in turn took care of her château on the banks of the Cher. Diane had had the five-arched bridge built across the river; now Catherine had the idea to top it with the three-storeyed gallery that made this structure, once it was touched up by Philibert Delorme, one of the most cheerful castles in the world.

V

In the midst of the lordly sixteenth century, dominated by the three great Ch's: delirious Chambord, rouged Chenonceau and frowning Chaumont, male and female, the Loire had become a building yard of wonders. Other girl-châteaux are Azay-le-Rideau on the river bank and Talcy to the north, which is lashed by the harsh wind of Beauce.

In *The Lily in the Valley* Balzac lingered at Azay. *"While climbing a hill, I admired for the first time the château of Azay, a facetted diamond set in the Indre and mounted on flower-masked piles."* It was his favorite. He had taste, because it is the most perfect. Azay delights by its location on the Indre, the harmony of this walls and roofs in their proportion and color, and that of the building and its reflection in the flowing water, for Azay is a château of running waters. It was the wife of a certain Gilles Berthelot, treasurer of France and mayor of Tours, who oversaw its construction, once more a product of the partnership between a financier and a pretty woman.

The park is the ideal place to read one of the *Droll Tales,* "How the Château of Azay Was Built". Here one finds nothing of the refined Balzac of *The Lily in the Valley* except the valley and nothing of the *Curate of Tours* and the realistic world of the author of *The Human Comedy* but a tale in which it would seem that Boccacio had inspired an author who wanted to pay hommage to his compatriot Rabelais.

Jacques de Beaune, a young Touraine burger, impecunious and very much put out by the disgrace of his father, Charles VIII's banker, meets a proud-looking woman out walking and notices her *"dress of Italian velvet, with big sleeves lined in satin"*. He follows her to her house and, as the admirer stays standing in front of her door, he receives a bucket of cold water, contents and container, on his head. He pretends to be dead. The compassionate lady is furious with her clumsy valet and has the young man seen after. Here he is inside the house. The lady of Beaujeu, daughter of Louis XI, Anne of France, moans in a remarkable spell of weakness: "Holy Easter! By the soul of my father, I'll have everyone hanged who has had a part in his death!" The rascal then jumps to his feet and *"looks at the good lady with an air that spoiled everything"*.

In short, and here we must imagine Balzac himself reading his parody, Anne lifted up the man from Touraine, and he *"proved by many a plea to his sovereign's ancient virtue that a lady bearing the burden of the state had the right to disport herself a little"*. To tell the truth, handsome Jacques had some qualities: if the dates are correct the austere and rough Madame la Grande was nearing sixty when the delightful château was built on the lands of the seigniory about 1518.

Flowers bloomed everywhere on terraces and orange trees spent the winter in green-houses. Villandry and its gardens became the park of the Map of Tenderness, a perfect example of amorous and gardening rhetoric. This happened around 1532, for the benefit of Jean Le Breton, secretary of state of King Francis. At Villandry, even the vegetable gardens obey drawing-pen and pruning shears! The layout of variously colored spots, according to the season, forms a graceful mosaic. As for the wonder of the place, the sculpted hedges, they are composed of coupled designs arranged in squares: plant and geometrical allegories. One finds there, in the form of living symbols, the themes that fascinated the authors of the *Romance of the Rose,* King René of Anjou and the Princess of Cleves. The drama of happiness is played out in four flower beds. Fans and butterflies incarnate happy love and its early beginnings. Next comes adultery: hearts and horns. Then the consequences: tears and daggers. Finally everything ends in the labyrinth of madness.

There was largely enough money to pay the contractors and masons, what with the trading due to the Italian wars, in this court of bankers, financiers, brokers, suppliers, painters as lavish as princes, enamellers, ceramists and jewelers (the Césars and Dalis of the time), profiteers of the war profiteers, arms manufacturers and even (already) land speculators. The intendance followed the princes!

In this novel of a thousand characters the most poetic chapter takes place at Talcy. Talcy rises on the other side of the golden river, between the Loire and the Loir, on the outskirts of Beauce. The outside of the castle is still markedly feudal, but it hides in its stone shell a courtyard made for courting, which is preciously ornamented with a pink and grey colonnaded gallery, a dovecote which is complete today except for the cooing, a wine press (this is still a land of vineyards), and a stone-curbed well, which is indeed the king of wells.

Around 1516, another Florentine, a cousin of the Medicis (yet another of the king's bankers by the grace of Catherine) built it. The golden-handed builder was Bernard Salviati. His name shows his origin.

Now, at a ball at the court of Blois, his daughter Cassandra, met the poet Ronsard. He was twenty-one and she sixteen.

Ronsard fell violently in love. True poet that he was, he did a good job of it. He wrote for her the 183 sonnets of the *Amours* and his most famous ode:

> *"Sweet, let us go see if the rose*
> *Which this morning opened*
> *Her robe of crimson to the sun*
> *Has not lost by this eventide*
> *The folds of her crimson robe*
> *And her color like your own.*

In those days on knew how to make compliments. And yet the result was disappointing. Cassandra married someone else.

Twenty years later, Cassandra was a widow and still beautiful when Ronsard returned to the well of Talcy. New wooing, new poem, new failure.

But Cassandra had a niece, another Diane. This was in 1571. Although the center of France was still between Orleans and Angers, times had become hard in a war without mercy. People were being disemboweled everywhere in the name of the true faith, and Touraine still lived in horror of the Amboise "tumult" and of the massacre of the spring of 1560, which was as terrible as the Parisian St. Bartholomew's Day, a massacre thus stigmatized by a young poet whom you would have taken for a bandit:

> *"The horrified kings grow pale and let drop*
> *From their bloody hands the reddening scepters."*

It was then that a young Huguenot leader arrived all bloody in the château of the new owner, Cassandra's brother and Diane's father, Jean Salviati. He was a tolerant Catholic, a fast-vanishing species, and he took in the wounded man. Alas, the wounded man was also a poet! And the Huguenot, author of the lines on Amboise, grew subdued under the tender care given him. Agrippa d'Aubigné took up Ronsard's lute near the well for the beautiful niece, dispatching this delightful madrigal accompanied by a mirror:

"You had asked me, my sweet,
For something new from Paris.
...Since I saw you I have seen nothing
That could be desired,
So I brought nothing back
Save this crystal I give you."

Unfortunately, she had an uncle who was a fierce papist. Agrippa had to flee. Diane, weary of it all, agreed to marry someone else; sometime later she once more saw Agrippa, who was by now married to Suzanne de Lezay, and died of sadness. As for Agrippa, he had never taken off the bracelet of braided golden hair given him by Diane Salviati.

Alfred de Musset was of this lineage. If only he had told the story of the roses of Talcy so that a French Verdi could have made a Valois opera of it.

It was at Tours about fifteen years ago in a bookstore located in what the Second World War had left of the old town. I was signing some of my books, among which *The Traveller of the Vale of the Loire,* when a very pretty woman stopped in front of me. By Francis, she was the Loire itself! Full-figured, graceful, painted by Primaticcio! And the light of her smile, as Eluard said! Her face was both oval and dimpled. Her eyes were the evening blue of Touraine and her hair was in artistically arranged tresses. I must have looked stupid with admiration, because she said in a slightly ironical tone:

"I don't know if you will accept to sign this volume for me, sir,"
"But Madame," I said, as stupidly as possible, *"that's why I'm here."*
"Oh, but you don't know my name." Her eyes sparkled more and more.
"My name is Babou de la Bourdaisière and I belong to the family you have said so many mean things about!"

One knows when one is blushing! I stuck my nose into my own book. It was worse than I had remembered! Page 81: *"From the beautiful Babou to da Vinci's frescoes."* This chapter treated Clos Lucé, near

Amboise, whose austere owner I had known, and who, I later learned, is the grandmother of our most romantic young contemporary, Gonzague St-Bris. I read: *"The funny thing is that this robust parishioner did not know that her house had belonged to a lady who was as famous as she was naughty. Before she herself had worn the keys of Clos Lucé at her waist, they had passed through the most frivolous hands, those of the beautiful Babou, Marie Babou de la Bourdaisière of whom Tallemant des Réaux said, that she "boasted of having slept not only with Francis I, but also with Pope Clement VII (another Medici!) and the Emperor Charles V'."*

"Continue! Don't you remember pages 96 and 97?"

This time, I must quote the entire passage. We are at Tours, near the house where Balzac was born and which was destroyed in 1940, at 8 Place Foire-le-Roi, at a hundred steps from the bookshop!

"You even give the addresses!"

She took the book and read: *"A splendid house calls to mind once again the beautiful Babou, professional éminence rose* (she made a face, all right), *daughter of Jean Babou de la Bourdaisière, superintendant of finances to Francis I and a blind (or complaisant) father.* (It's between parentheses in your text! So you are the one who says it!) *The beautiful Babou and her six sisters were called the seven deadly sins: they were a pretty herd of does who were easy to force.* (Another one of your remarks!) *So Marie, Countess of Saint-Aignan (the beautiful Babou) and her sisters, including Madeleine, Diane and Françoise.* (I'll find the Christian names of the three others for you.) *The family of these ravishing ladies of Touraine was from Bourdaisière... Marie was the scandalous one of Clos Lucé. Françoise deserves special mention.* (Another grimace.) *Françoise d'Estrées was to become the mother of the beautiful Gabrielle, Gabrielle d'Estrées, mistress of Henry IV.* (She slowed her speech, which became sheer delectation.) *It seems that a courtesan's qualities are more easily transmitted from mother to daughter than poetry, painting or even music!* How should I take that, Mister Author, especially when you end this deed of derring-do (that is what one calls it, isn't it?) by a quotation from Tallemant des Réaux: *La Bourdaisière was the most fertile family for producing "light women" that ever was in France."*

Crushed, I contented myself with drawing a rose and signing my name on the end-paper.

She walked out like the mistress of a king.

Since then I have reread the file. Well, it was worse than I had said! If I ever see the last of the Babous, I will gladly complete the dedication: "I have reread, I persist and I sign."

VI

In spite of the Italian influence, even though one finds châteaux everywhere in the Vale of the Loire, there is no *palazzo*. The *palazzo* hardly exists north of Aix-en-Provence, Aix of the paradoxical René of Anjou, the uprooted king. In spite of its infinite diversity the château is not a palace in the Italian style. Its spirit is more temperate, less *commedia dell'arte*. The baroque does not flow over the outer walls of Chambord. Of course, there are other lordly regions in France: granite Brittany, Ile-de-France sprinkled with small Louis XIII houses whose pink brick shines behind the grey curtains of poplars, as in Nerval, Périgord and Auvergne, frowning superbly, but the prize goes to the Loire from its source to Saint-Nazaire.

But precisely which Loire? The hunch-backed France of the river's beginnings has the right to claim its child, from its source on Mount Gerbier-de-Jonc! Certain geographers who love paradox even think that it is by a real misappropriation that the Loire is so-called, when it is in reality the Allier, as the Seine would be the Yonne. Its birthplace would be in Lozère at Mourre de la Gardille and not at Prébachard. In this new geography, the Allier and the Yonne flow into the Atlantic! Water games? Word games? Yes, of course, but of the thousands of kilometers of its course, how many belong to the part of the Valley the French call the Vale? The Vale has monopolized the name and topography is defeated by semantics. Very well. Where then does the Vale begin and where does it stop? The French National Railway, geologists, poets, cooks and paleographers all have different ideas on the subject. And they are right: any decision will be arbitrary. Just as there is no break between the hall of the Estates of the château of Blois and the more recent buildings constructed by Mansard for Gaston of Orleans, the cheat, so we shall not find a single one between the Orleanais, land of vinegar and wind, and black Anjou which is sown with menhirs. I have ended up treating it like an omelette: I cut off both ends, the Breton and the Auvergnat. What's left is our Vale of the Loire.

No part of the French hexagon of our grade school maps is as feminine as this admirable region. It is like a warmed-up goddess by Jean Goujon. She stands lightly, one foot on each bank, at Pouilly and at Sancerre, the exquisite tip of the wine district, one of her feet extending beyond the other just the length of a pearly toe. The dainty calves curve between Gien and Orleans, and the thighs lie lazily, like those of Diane of Poitiers, between Orleans and Blois, but they are those of Diana the Huntress whose arrows slew more hearts than deer.

As a matter of fact, the Vale of the Loire begins at Gien, whose inhabitants claim the first castle rebuilt in 1484 by Anne of France, the heroine of the tale we read at Azay-le-Rideau, "the least silly woman in France, for I do not know of a wise one."

From Gien on, the Loire, weary of flowing north by northwest, slants towards the northwest. At Orleans it turns ninety degrees to larboard! It heads due west, then west by southwest. Now it has only to idle along between its levees and reflect its castles.

Between Blois and Saumur, the body swells into a curve whose sensuality becomes more refined but is still quite visible. And as if by chance, to illustrate this poem of the female body, there flourish all along in history beautiful favorites from the Blesois and Touraine who compete for the honor of being the model for our river nymph.

The perfect torso of this *éminence rose* swells into full curves between Touraine and Anjou, where the throat of the Loire coos like a dove. This is indeed Anjou, whose mere name is like a compliment! Isn't it enough to tell a woman she is Angevine to make her blush? Try it.

Then her neck, which is long, as the Renaissance canon of beauty demands, bends under the weight of sleep and the lazy head falls on the pillow of the estuary, the nape of her neck in the sand, bathing in the running water which reflects the purest of all French skies.

28

It is true that there is a light common to all these regions, which gives them unity and which is not the same once you leave them. There is a light of the Loire just as there is a light of Provence or a light of Ile-de-France. It would take a lifetime to give consistence to ideas based on things intangible. And yet, the light of the Loire is precisely the one that a few miniaturists and their master, Jean Fouquet, have captured in their gouache paintings highlighted in gold, just as the light of the Seine is that of the Impressionists.

From Orleans to Angers, it bathes stones and ivy, brambles and gardens. It organizes into enchanted recitals all the celebrated castles, but also these more modest houses of happiness, the Béchellerie of Anatole France, the Grenadière of Balzac and the Gaudinière of Bergson, handsome houses without which the picture would lack a middle-class resonance.

VII

Yes, the Vale is Valois.

If one had to affirm the particular charm emanating from the Loire in fifteen letters and four words, those are the ones I would choose. This is not simple acrobatics of language. The Loire is indeed an historical valley of a French subtlety that did not exist in the Middle Ages and that was to disappear with the arrogant ostensory of the Sun King.

The great Couperin, a Parisian originally from the Ile-de-France, author of the admirable *Lessons of Darkness,* used the well-tempered harpsichord. Let's rid the word of its technical meaning and give it back the plain music of words. The Valois Vale, from the lute to the harpsichord, gave an uninterrupted concert for two and a half centuries, well-tempered in its skies and in its castles: a lesson in light.

The typical product of the Vale is thus indeed the castle or château. The castle began to rise out of the earth practically during the Neolithic age, at the time when the woman preferred to sow and reap rather than to follow hordes of game or even herds of cattle. Adam was a hunter, Eve was to be a shepherdess and cattlewoman. Is this ancient history? Yes, on the European continent, but the America of the western tells the same saga, and it is less than a hundred years old! It was not Calamity Jane who dominated with her horse and her Colts, but the emigrant woman who got off the Wild Wild West train. In the Loire, she established the family. The castle appeared. In the United States, there has not been time. Manhattan sprang up right away!

Oh, let's admit it, it was hard to get it out of the ground! The living rooms and the winemaker's cellars (one began very early to make wine) were hidden in the rock. A chimney was made in the limestone for heating purposes. Soon came the wheel, the horse and the consumer civilization! It happens that Raboliot cooked his stew over the fire of dried deer dung of the twice-robbed lord. This underground lodging of constant temperature remained tiny. The sedentary woman wanted room. So the lord dug or rather he had others dig!

What could be done with the debris when the stone came out in handsome blocks of white gold? One piled it up outside in the manner of certain shepherd's folds, with no other cement than mud from the river. But while they were at it, they evened up the rough terrain. These spontaneous walls which came out of the cave like the claws of a hermit-crab, why not make holes in them in order to see the enemy and the sunset in the distance? Just a moment of absent-mindedness and architecture was invented!

Cave-dwelling reigns almost everywhere on the banks of the Loire and its tributaries, whether at Bléré on the Cher, or at Trôo in the Loir Valley or at Chinon. One might even mention a charming castle, between Chançay and Reugny, that of Côte, which emerges from the cave like the house of the Vouvray winemaker where one enters the cellars through a trick wardrobe.

Here, as well as at Ussé, the true castle of the sleeping beauty, one can easily see how the castle came to be built on the hillside. Necessity is the mother of invention. Invaders came from all directions! This building is first of all a fortress. The progression of toolmaking, the increase in manpower and the passage from the ancient pastoral society to the feudal one drew the castle toward the military keep.

The bored look-outs in their coats of mail would see the arrival of Bretons and Normans, the English bristling with lances, and Arab horsemen, not to speak of Huns! The castle crinkled its eyes of stone until they became mere slits too small to let an arrow pass. The thickness of its walls tripled and they were surrounded with moats trembling with frogs which probably did not keep the lord from sleeping. Wearing sixty pounds of iron fifteen hours a day must have made the knight drop into a deep sleep at once! Only the lady of the manor heard the frogs. The trouveres were to follow. I said trouveres, for there were no troubadours here. They did not come this far north, even in the wake of the lady who invented courtly love, Alienor of Aquitaine. On the Loire, *oc* was never used in place of *oui*. *Oil* was. Garlic is not eaten, but shallots and onions are. No olive oil, but walnut oil, which is not to be sneezed at, and above all sweet butter, almost as much of it as among the Normans. Ask the chefs of Anjou, Touraine and the Orleanais for the recipe for "white butter". You'll copy it down scrupulously and you'll not be able to make it!

VIII

Slowly, war moved away from the happy river. To tell the truth, it was being fought a little further on among the Turks because of the Crusades preached by St. Bernard, who was as ardent to hunt the Moor as he was to fight the first existentialist, Abelard. The most joyous campaigns took place in Italy.

The Valois kings had hereditary rights over the kingdom of Naples and the Duchy of Milan. Charles VIII claimed them and won one victory, but he hit his head against the lintel of a door and died from it, the prototype of what is commonly called a stupid accident, as if there were smart ones. His successors, Louis XII and Francis I, continued. They didn't conquer Italy, but the Italians, who were in fact defeated, occupied the Vale of the Loire. The king brought back Medicis, da Vincis, a cohort of financiers, Bernard Palissys and Primaticcios, engineers and astrologers, not to mention the "Italian disease" which the Italians call the "French disease".

Naturally, old Leonardo, prince of harmony, looked at the feudal buildings with a severe eye. He appreciated them as an engineer, but he had little taste for this bestial accumulation of machicolations. The feudal being out of style, how could one demolish these thick walls? or build next door? All the best sites were taken! A solution was soon found. The outside of the fortress would not be changed. And then, one never knew, the Arabs and the English might return! The inner façades had large mullioned windows that opened onto exquisite courtyards where the curbstone of a well crumbled under the rose and the ivy and where Ronsard's doves cooed.

The Renaissance flourished in the shell of feudalism. Why Renaissance? Out of snobbery. The word was justified in Italy, which returned to its origins, but was it so in France where there had been nothing but druids, bards and dolmens? This was of no importance. The word caught on. The University took it up. Scholars wrote theses about it. The trend was irreversible. Blois, Tours, Chambord, Chenonceau, Azay-le-Ridel and two hundred others took a new form.

This time France chose its epicenter, which for once was just about in the center of the kingdom! The Valois had been governing since 1328. Louis XI's capital was Tours. This was to last until the Edict of Nantes in 1598, two and a half centuries during which the Valois princes dropped like flies in the convulsions of religious wars and hereditary diseases. Catherine gave Henry II more reigning kings than the best mare, but they all died! It began with Francis II, the eldest, a pale sovereign whom we remember as looking like a sickly choirboy. He died at the age of sixteen, having theoretically reigned one year. Charles IX, the second son, who was drawn by François Clouet, succeeded him. He lasted fourteen years, with Catherine as regent, and then died at twenty-four. Henry III succeeded him. He was to endure a little longer, thirty-seven years, of which fifteen years of reign. Catherine's favorite was afflicted with malaria, the Valois malady. A decadent breed. A fine June night in 1577, at Chenonceau, he was celebrating with the Florentine the victory of his brother François d'Alençon, over the Huguenots. The orgy lasted all night. The king wore a pink and silver dress (yes, a dress). *And each person was hard put to say whether he saw a woman king or a man queen.* All the guests were dressed in green, the men disguised as women and vice versa. Green was the color of jesters.

Henry had no heir because he was too busy playing cup-and-ball. When the jovial Henry IV figured that Paris was well worth a mass, everything was over. The transvestite comedy of Chenonceau was finished. A strong odor of garlic flooded over France.

Forsaken by kings and their *éminences roses,* the Loire went to sleep. The politics of France, which was becoming unified, were being acted out on other shores. The Italian influence, *fa presto* and *la dolce vita* were done with! A revolution had taken place in two phases, the first being the pacification desired by Henry IV by means of the Edict of Nantes, the second the revocation of the Edict in 1685, a movement whose consequences for the Loire were the same: desertion. By abjuring, Henry IV brought a new idea to the Western world, that of religious freedom. But he also reinforced the Protestant party, and, at the same time, he went against the current of monarchic centralization.

A precarious balance lasted until October 1685. Worried by the general weakenning of a divided nation, Richelieu and then Louis XIV strove for unity. It was the red cardinal and the Sun King who created the future Jacobin spirit of a State one and indivisible.

More military and political and even geopolitical than religious, Richelieu was not mistaken in his analyses. He feared the forces that were tending to break up France, which was not yet a nation and which was encircled by a hostile Europe. One must see the relentlessness he manifested against Cinq-Mars and which was so strongly stressed by Vigny in his novel *Cinq-Mars or a Conspiracy under Louis XIII.*

At Cinq-Mars-la-Pile two towers are still standing to bear witness to this tragedy. Cinq-Mars, Henri Coiffier de Ruzé, a marquess, was born in 1620. Louis XIII, who loved him very much, too much perhaps, had made him Master of the Horse. Richelieu reigned in fact. Cinq-Mars fell in love with Marie de Gonzague, a princess. The cardinal, who looked unfavorably upon the king's preference for this marquess, opposed the marriage. Urged on by his beautiful, ambitious mistress, Cinq-Mars negotiated with Spain. During this period, the nobility saw nothing wrong in obtaining the aid of foreigners in order to maintain its privileges or attain its ends. Loyalty to caste prevailed over patriotism. The concept of collaboration with the enemy had not yet been formed.

Richelieu detested the nobles' lack of discipline and their symbolic castles. This was all the more true as he owned only a wretched paternal manor-house in the Richelais, on the border of Touraine and Poitou. Ten years after the execution of Henri de Montmorency at Toulouse, in 1632, the plot of young Cinq-Mars broke out into the open. The king was hesitant. Richelieu was to say that the four square feet of the king's study were more difficult to guard than all the battlefields of Europe! Louis XIII dropped his equerry, due to weakness or purposely, when he saw the treaty the favorite had signed with the people from beyond the Pyrenees. Cinq-Mars was executed at Lyons, along with his friend de Thou, whose only crime was that of not denouncing the plot. And the castle of Cinq-Mars was razed *to the height of infamy*. Cinq-Mars was twenty-two years old.

In her memoirs, Madame de Motteville denounced the magnitude of the plot, which proved that although the cardinal was unforgiving, he was not without political genius. *"The king was tacitly part of the conspiracy. The great Cinq-Mars was the soul of it, the name used being that of the Duke of Orleans, the king's only brother."* This had far-reaching implications. And even more far-reaching in the case of the cardinal, since the admitted object of the plot was his assassination. Without having really understood what had happened to him, Cinq-Mars said, just before the axe fell: "My God, what is the world?" The question still applies.

Richelieu, who had built an almost Cartesian villa in Touraine, at Richelieu itself, preferred the middle class to those undisciplined princes and it was with pleasure that he saw Touraine and Anjou become covered with houses and rich residences belonging to merchants and persons of distinction. From this time on, the Loire has been only a region of whimsies that awake it for a few days at long intervals. Louis XIV returning from the Pyrenees stopped at Chambord with Maria Theresa. He admired Francis's petrified dream and acknowledged it. In the guardroom, which had been turned into a theater, in October 1670, the king applauded the *Bourgeois Gentilhomme,* that forerunner of the *Barber of Seville.* But the project of having Chambord restored by Mansard was given up because of the bills for Versailles. King Stanislas of Poland was lodged there and also Field Marshal Maurice de Saxe, who camped there with his Mongol guards. Napoleon was to make a caserne of it. The Restoration gave it to the Duke of Bordeaux (the one who was so much like his father). During this period a vine-grower of La Chavonnière, near Tours, wrote with an acid-dipped pen: *"Here, Louis, paragon of kings, lived with the Montespan woman, the La Vallière girl and and all the women and girls that his good pleasure caused him to take away from their husbands."*

Paul-Louis Courier paid for this with two months in prison.

In 1873 France, which had for a half-century hesitated between monarchy and republic, offered the crown to a descendant of the Bourbons, the Count of Chambord. The affair appeared to be settled, the two royalist clans, the modern Orleans one and the integrist Bourbon one, having finally agreed on a single pretender. The coaches were freshly gilded for the official entrance into Paris, when it all fell through, with the Count of Chambord clinging tooth and nail to the white flag with the fleur-de-lys. The coaches stayed in the stables.

They are still there.

IX

Of course, building went on after the Valois: spick and span Cheverny, which, although it was finished in 1634, was already of the majestic proportions of the Louis XIV style, and Ménars, north of the river, which was the last of the Loire castles. We have again an *éminence rose*, the Poisson woman, Antoinette, born of a prevaricator and a prostitute, alias Madame Pompadour. She had more taste than virtue; this can be seen at Champs in the Ile-de-France, as well as at Ménars, between Cléry and Blois, an old corbelled château for which she hired Gabriel and Soufflot in 1760. The château was barely finished when Cotillion IV, as Frederick of Prussia called her, died, on April 15, 1764. Louis XV, who was no longer the Beloved, would no longer come to feed the carps in the fish-pond near the temple of Love.

It was during the rather morbid sagging of a society that a dramatic turn of events occurred and there where it was least expected, as this sort of thing should be. In 1647, was born at Blois, not far from Catherine's delightful château and that of Ruggieri, the poison cabinet and the assassination of the Duke de Guise, a boy with a name like that of a Balzac character. The Papins were Protestants. They were to emigrate when the

Edict of Nantes was revoked. One of their children, Denis, who was an engineer and a physicist, had as a boy much observed the household cooking pot, whose lid rose and fell with the boiling of the liquid inside. Cooking pot lids had, of course, been rising up at the height of children's noses for a long time, but no one had observed them very closely, it seems, no more than before Newton anyone had seen apples fall. Denis had a good eye, and that changed the world.

One should beware of cooking pots. One never knows what is simmering in them. Pandora was in that one, an industrial Pandora! Domesticated steam was to be as important as the future gasoline engine bursting from Aladdin's oil lamp. But the little Touraine engineer went further than his pressure cooker. An energetic devil, on the basis of his steam engine he made a paddle-wheel steamboat.

What had he thought up now? Everything was going to change in one man's lifetime, the carriage of goods by boat, fishing, houses, markets and transportation! Soon the Loire was covered with flat-bottomed boats whose smoke gave a taste of coal-dust to the wines of Vouvray, Bourgueil and Chinon. The word "pollution" did not exist then, but the fact was evident. The Loire with its moving bottom was encumbered with these "Unexplodables" with their mustaches of smoke, which plied the river from Nantes to Orleans and back. The soft-water sailors with a gold ring in one ear sang at the top of their voices:

> Let's sing of the Loire and its navy,
> On land nothing can compare,
> On the road to the sunrise...

Balzac and Hugo as well as folk songs bear witness to this popular bantering Loire of the sailors. The boatman holding his boat-hook or stiffening the sail in the west wind has become one of the main images of historical films.

The adventure story of the Loire has the most classical features of the novel. The unity of setting is strengthened by the idea of its being the "garden of France". The unity of time is that of the Valois domination.

Last, the unity of action brings everything together in a single plot: the conquest of a territory by man and the disintegration of this empire.

This is due to the fact that soon after Papin, other "geniuses of the cooking pot" were to be swallowed up! In two decades, the conflict between river fleet and railroad was decided. The Loire and its fleets, which still prevailed around 1830, were to leave the stage. Thirteen years were enough for the iron horse, still run by steam, to come to Orleans, Tours and Nantes! The river, ruined once again, returned lazily to its banks and filled up with silt.

But history doesn't stop. Although the Loire experienced without too many changes the heroic defense of Gambetta's armies in 1871, then the human sacrifices of World War I, then the lamentable and bloody crossing of the bombed bridges in June 1940, and the defense of Saumur and Montoire, other germs were being slyly introduced.

The most important today is the construction of buildings. Everywhere identical pencil boxes are being built on the outskirts of historic towns, choking them with concrete. In parallel fashion the dams on the Upper-Loire, the necessary transformation of levees into dikes, the dredges which change the course of the river, all demonstrate the menaces of the late twentieth century. Quarries have increased in number. The mechanism is simple. One makes concrete with sand and gravel, so the cement that comes out of the Loire threatens it, as if, once again, the river was secreting the poisons that destroy it.

In 1978, when Maurice Genevoix was interviewed during a television program concerning great rivers, he made a startling remark. Comparing the fish-filled Loire of this childhood to the river of today, he used this image: "The Loire trembles no more." Are the waters already dead?

Twenty years ago the Loire differed little from Balzac's river. In these twenty years everything has changed! Almost everywhere tall impersonal buildings have perverted the relationship between water and sky. But the Loire is harmony within a measured space. The planners spoke of a garden-metropolis. Is this project, which is already frightening in inself, still possible? Should it all be halted now? Time flows like a river and life does not allow zero economic growth. Only one point seems positive: the words *ecology, quality of life, environment* and *natural harmony* had very little meaning in 1950. Today they carry more weight. This is the last hope for the Loire.

What has become of *heritage* itself, the last semantic invention, in 1980, of governmental power that knows very well how to make words serve its needs? The châteaux, pride of the Vale, are threatened. Like England, Italy and all countries rich in history, France *produces* a considerable number of "endangered masterpieces".

During the seventeenth and even more during the eighteenth century, castles passed into the hands of the middle class, and during the Revolution, into those of stewards. But in the face of their high upkeep, the latter gave them up in turn. Hens came to lay their eggs in the guardrooms and the tiles fell.

This development was due as much to indifference as to poverty, with fashion veering toward Paris after Versailles, such being the course of history. In the middle of the nineteenth century, the love of the past having followed the romantic movement, owners began to restore. But since then, economic pressure has been a factor, the result of a costly civilization. The cutting up of estates has finished the job. Few great castles still belong to individuals and there are no more than two still belonging to the families that built them, Cheverny and Brissac, at the western limits of the Vale. Patrons of the arts having disappeared, "endangered masterpieces" can be saved only by the state, which is crushed under the weight of so many costly inheritances, by towns for reasons of prestige (but they are usually not rich) and by tourism.

So castles take to the road, as in René Clair's film, *The Ghost Goes West!* Foreign companies raid the non-classified residences, in particular those of Viollet-le-Duc's time, still known as the Gothic Revival, a fashion that was the baroque of the nineteenth century, starting with Alexandre Dumas, who followed the fashion in his manor-house of Monte Cristo near Paris and ending with Robida's reconstitutions for the Exhibition of 1900 and its celebrated *Manor-house in Reverse.* In 1979 four Anjou castles were thus packed into crates and exported!

Is this the end for the river of sand and sky? The threat is not negligeable. Of course, for the tourist and even for the lucky owner of a country home, the Vale of the Loire is still the paradise of a certain happy mannerism. The air there has something of both the south and the ocean. You feel that the sea is not far away. And the countryside is fruitful: grapes, plums, peaches, the melons Ronsard liked, walnuts and even truffles! The markets of Tours abound with garden fruits. In spite of industrialization, concrete silos sprung up from the wheatfields of the *Book of the Enamoured Heart,* the fact that Saumur, Orleans and Blois are spoiled by new suburbs and that even Chambord is threatened, the Vale's magic is still evident, based as it is on the poetry of trouveres and music for ladies and unicorns. And all that is due to the magic of light.

In his *Droll Tales,* Balzac evokes Tours in the language of Rabelais: *"How true it is that Tours has had and will always have her feet in the Loire, like a pretty girl bathing and playing with the water, going splish splash while whipping up the water with her white hands..."*

Can one think like Balzac that the Loire will always be this beautiful girl? The bridges are tottering and the salmon refuse to climb the ladders in the locks.

The sun sets beyond Ponts-de-Cé, at Jules Verne's. Will it inevitably take with it to the land of the green ray the millenary lament of my sister the Loire? I prefer to look for the moral of the story in Paul Fort's works about his Touraine beauty:

"Happiness is in the meadow,
Run there fast, run there fast,
Happiness is in the meadow,
Run there fast, it's going to slip away."

Listen to See If It's Raining.

Armand Lanoux.

The Vale of the Loire
as the water flows

by
Annie Cospérec

To my brother, Jean-François Guénolé

WRITING after so many others on the château country of the Loire, I want simply to retrace my own steps as I have discovered the region by wandering through it during the last few years.

But is the Vale of the Loire, which is so difficult to pinpoint, really a district or region or is it rather a succession of small provincial entities jealously turned inward on themselves? Be that as it may, a secret unity, a mysterious bond, connects them all: the broad-valleyed Loire whose slow, majestic course is enriched from Tours to Angers by a network of large tributaries. These pages will be above all a walk through the unknown or poorly known parts of the Vale of the Loire. Their guiding line is the course of the river and its tributaries and the many little streams that drain the plateau. We shall wander as the water flows and in no way follow a precise itinerary or make a methodical catalogue of curiosities. To appreciate these regions whose beauty is synonymous with moderation and quiet poetry, we must accept to waste our time. The great châteaux, which are justly famous, and the much-travelled circuits overshadow the many more modest structures: manor-houses, country homes of the gentry and abbeys which I want you to discover.

To visit the Vale you must be intelligently lazy and leave the beaten paths to choose winding lanes with unexpected byways. A certain slowness is also necessary to be able to appreciate the beauty of a region as delicately varied as the light reflected off stone and water against a background of forests. This uncommon luminosity is of incomparable lightness and delicately emphasizes the whiteness of the tufa buildings, particularly in Touraine, where this white and creamy stone with a delicate, soft texture, gives the most modest home a touch of class.

Avoiding the traditional chronological limits which confine the art of the Loire too strictly within the Renaissance, I prefer to treat the whole artistic heritage. The medieval period has left enough evidence to show the continuity of a tradition in the art of building, and the Loire Renaissance would not have had such luster without this local know-how. I also like to think that kings and princes did not come to the Vale of the Loire only because of historical circumstances but were charmed by the beauty of the region. Its moderation and grace have nothing of the grandiose austerity of mountainous regions or the lavishness of seascapes. The Vale of the Loire is one of the most melancholy regions in the world and also one of the most attractive; only care-worn persons will find it monotonous.

Nonetheless, the atmosphere of the Loire cannot be captured in a few words, because it escapes definition: it may be the golden clarity of a summer evening when the sun meets the river as it sets. You must then be quiet, stop on a levee, lean against the parapet of a bridge and soak up this light. But can you sum up the region you love in the sun's brightness and a few beads of water?

The Loire Valley
Orleanais . Blesois . Touraine . Anjou

The Orleanais

Now nonchalant in its meanderings among the islands of golden sand, now ardent and grey with sometimes tumultuous waves, the Loire can sparkle too. When it enters the Orleanais it turns once and for all westward, seaward, flowing through the middle of a broad valley bordered by two rows of low hills.

Between Briare and Ozouer, the Loire enters a large hollow which it crosses slowly, making a large loop as it flows toward Touraine. The Valley is then bordered by small hills, and levees begin to appear, earthwork dikes which protect it from high water. These few features are constantly to be seen in the Loire Valley landscape from the Orleanais to Anjou.

On one of these hills which announce those of the Blesois and Touraine, the château of Gien looks like a sentinel standing at the gateway to the Vale. In spite of its strategic position, there is nothing of the fortress about it. Rebuilt at the end of the fifteenth century by the daughter of Louis XI, Anne de Beaujeu, it is rather an agreeable country house with its turrets, and the living quarters with polychrome walls are made of red and black bricks set together in geometric designs of great variety.

At Gien the Loire begins to broaden, washing further along the towers of the château of Sully which was built in the middle of a pond fed by the river. To the east, as you travel away from the Vale, you enter the rich Orleanais countryside where market gardens alternate with copses. Bellegarde, a big, square keep, appears then among the orchards, half-castle, half-fortress, flanked by corbelled towers. In the shadow of the austere ramparts, the village church is embellished with a Romanesque porch. In the neighboring countryside, at the bend in a lane, the château of La Bussière, in the middle of a pond, jealously preserves its solitude behind a screen of greenery. These few buildings alone evoke the atmosphere of the Loire Valley: castle reflected in the water, medieval keep, Romanesque church and manor-house hidden in the woods.

The region of Orleans is not yet really the land of châteaux, in spite of the structures that mark the Valley road. The abbey of Saint-Benoît-on-Loire, by its influence and prestige, eclipses the few examples of secular architecture around Orleans. This abbey of Fleury took the name of Saint-Benoît (St. Benedict) dear to the Capetians in the seventh century and then became a famous place of pilgrimage. Royal protection favored its growth and the rise of its school of manuscripts during all the medieval period.

The major part of the present structure was rebuilt in the twelfth century. The abbatial church is flanked by a big tower which you enter through an immense porch. Upon entering you are struck by the majesty of the structure. The inside, a belfry-porch of colossal size, contrasts with the slender proportions of the ambulatory. A series of capitals which are among the most beautiful of Romanesque sculpture ennoble the porch and the church. Scenes from the Old Testament, revelations and the Last Judgement are associated with an exuberant and fanciful decoration of flora and fauna.

St. Benedict's abbey is still today one of those places of meditation and peace unaltered by the centuries. Its unassuming neighbor, the church of Germigny of the Fields, although entirely rebuilt in the last century, is one of the most ancient religious edifices in France. A mosaic of deep blues lining the vault of the apse is the only vestige of the Carolingian church. This sanctuary is now shaded by a flowering garden of tamarisk trees and hollyhocks.

A little further on, before you reach Orleans, Chateauneuf-on-Loire is worth a visit because the museum collections are devoted to the navy of the Loire. Those nostalgic for the days when the Loire was navigated will discover a fine retrospective! Although the château has disappeared, the park at least remains and alone is worth a visit, preferably in May when the flowering rhododendrons are the inspiration for a popular festival. The mildness of the Loire Valley climate allows the growing of plant species that usually grow only in more southerly regions.

The proximity of Paris has made Orleans the largest city of the Vale.

Already protected by the Capetians who gave it a privileged place, it rapidly became a religious, political and intellectual metropolis of medieval France. Many monuments bore witness to this illustrious past: cathedrals, churches, mansions and houses, many of which have vanished. Orleans has suffered a great deal from the ignorance of human beings, the destructions during the nineteenth century due to the war and the changes brought about by its role as regional capital, in particular.

Here and there in the steets, between modern structures, you can still discover a few beautiful façades and a few intact houses, which have often been transformed into museums. The former city hall, built of brick and stone, whose flamboyant Gothic decoration reminds one of a Flemish house, and several Renaissance mansions such as the curious house of Oves, the Cabu mansion and the Colas des Francs pavillion, are the rare examples that bear witness to the extraordinary wealth of the city.

On the road from Orleans to Blois, as you leave Chapelle-Saint-Martin, a lane of great trees leads to a château hidden in a tall forest: Ardoise, built in the eighteenth century on the site of a feudal keep. On a broad terrace one overlooks the Vale, which looks very much as it has since Gien: the river bordered with woods runs there, silent and solitary, its waters broken by sandbanks. It flows thus under Meung, a burg buried in the greenery of its gardens and brought back to life by a stream. The low houses drowse around a church which is curiously shored up by a ruined tower. Nearby, a small sixteenth-century castle is hidden by trees. Together with a city gate, this is all that remains of the Meung-on-Loire of former times. On this spot abides the memory of two poets: Jean de Meung, lord of the fief, who added 18,000 lines to the *Romance of the Rose,* and one of worse reputation but who was much more "modern", François Villon, who was, it is said, imprisoned in the keep by order of the bishop of Orleans.

On the other side of the Loire, opposite Meung, Cléry-Saint-André is famous for its church which was built in the second half of the fifteenth century by Louis XI. Contrary to royal tradition, he wanted to be buried in this church, a masterpiece of flamboyant art. On the right bank, Beaugency, like Meung-on-Loire, still looks like a fortified blockhouse commanding the Loire; a few ruined buildings and some old houses remind us of its warlike past. The tiered town on a hillside above the river forms a homogenous whole and is perfectly integrated with the countryside; it is remarkable for its simplicity of line. The site is crowned with an enormous square keep: Caesar's tower.

The keep is now only a stone skeleton, crushing by its mass the small castle nearby which was built by Dunois in the fifteenth century. Rather austere, it has nonetheless beautiful façades on the inner courtyard which are embellished with dormer windows and a small polygonal turret containing a staircase.

Curtains of poplars trembling in the wind, islands of greenery and tongues of bare sands, verdant hills and chalky cliffs, these same landscapes succeed one another from Orleans to Blois with a somewhat monotonous regularity. But that is the charm of flat lands which can be taken in in a single look.

The Blesois

From Beaugency to Blois, a vast plateau overlooks the right bank of the Loire, announcing the open fields of Beauce. Here the river knocks against the wooded cliff of this plateau, while the other bank opens onto the marshy, forested horizons of Sologne.

In Beauce big rural burgs gather around their stocky bell-towers. The great château of Avaray, which was built in the eighteenth century, is rustic and stern, like the surrounding countryside. In this part of the Blesois nothing yet foretells the luxury and refinement of the châteaux of the Loire if not a manor-house that allies simplicity and grace: Talcy. This château rises on the church square in the middle of the village. The outside is austere but the courtyard, which is more welcoming, announces the art of the Loire. On the side of the fields and the village a thick stone keep, more honorary than defensive, props up the porch through which one enters the courtyard. It is closed by the two wings of the main building, one of which opens onto a little gallery with segmented arcades. The attics are lighted by highly curved dormer windows without any sort of decoration; a small polygonal turret which houses a spiral staircase, is next to the keep. There is nothing very elaborate in this arrangement, which is closer to a manor-house than to a château, and many details still remind us of life in the fields. In the unevenly paved courtyard, a slate-domed, columned well-house is the only luxury of this residence without frills. A few trees, wild flowers and an orchard behind the outbuildings separate the manor-house from the fields of wheat all around. And yet Talcy is more than a simple manor-house: it is the symbol of a way of life; beautiful Cassandra, celebrated by Ronsard, was born here.

As we return to the road to Blois we see Ménars spread out over a high hill, facing the Loire, with its long regular façade and its terraced gardens in front. One enters the château through a large courtyard to arrive at the Louis XIII main building, flanked by two projecting wings. A steep slate roof broken by pedimented dormer windows crowns the whole. On the terraces, in the center of the majestic façade is a double staircase which leads to the gardens. One enters by two flights of stairs whose ends are embellished by griffins with heads of women. Steps lead to the terraces overlooking the river. Everywhere here hovers the gracious memory of the Marquise de Pompadour.

Near Blois, one must make a detour toward the marches of Sologne, a strange region, which is very different from the Vale and its light. The white tufa stone is no longer to be seen. The castles that mark the course of the Cosson are of brick. The "Fertés", such as Ferté-Saint-Cyr, Ferté-Beauharnais and Ferté-Imbault, were rebuilt in the seventeenth and eighteenth centuries.

One edifice, however, does not show this regularity. Built on the border of this marshy region, Chambord ressembles Sologne only in its wooded surroundings. So much has been written on its architecture, its history and its exceptional surroundings that it is useless to add to the list. I would simply like to evoke here the impression I had as an adolescent when I discovered it. Chambord appeared like a phantom castle, hidden in the heart of an immense forest. The white façades standing out against the dark line of the woods, the teeming towers, domes, lantern-lights, chimmeys and dormer windows sparkling in the sun- it all seemed like a mirage!

This castle seemed to me marked with a strange melancholy. The result of a prince's whim, it seemed desperately empty, abandoned as soon as it was built, like an uninhabitable dream. One would have thought that an enchantment held it there in the depths of this loneliness, far from the royal river which should have mirrored it. Only later did I understand the symbolic value of Chambord whose very simple structure is organized around the enormous staircase. It was conceived as the ideal palace by a humanistic prince and, in order to be great, it had to ramain uninhabitable so that nothing would alter the relationship of the volumes created by the strict plan. All that mattered were the double spiral staircase at the center of the cross-shaped floor plan, and the contrast between the bareness of the façades and the exuberant richness of the upper parts.

The enchantment of Chambord is to be found nowhere else in Sologne. Not far away, a stream, the Beuvron, washes the park of Villesavin. Built around 1537 by Jean Le Breton, Villesavin is one of the finest residences in the Blesois. It has remained almost completely intact to the present time and is composed of a ground floor topped with a large attic lighted by pedimented dormer windows with concave ramps. Although it belongs to the Loire school by the disposition of its façades and the style of its capitals, its buildings are already arranged in the classical style. The substitution of square pavilions for corner towers disposes the wings of the building around an open courtyard and gives it the character of a country house.

A few leagues from there the Beuvron washes also the park of the château of Beauregard, hidden by the great trees of Russy forest. Built between 1545 and 1550 and remodelled the following century, it is known to the public for its gallery of seventeenth century portraits. You shouldn't forget, however, the Renaissance structure, of which there remains only one wing at the back of the main courtyard. The well-balanced proportions of this building are emphasized by the sobriety and refinement of the decoration, making up a homogenous whole which has been

48

somewhat marred by unfortunate additions made during the last century.

From Beauregard you arrive at Blois by the left bank of the Loire in the suburb of Vienne, opposite the old stone bridge. You must approach the city from this side in order to see in its entirety the superb view of the buildings set in tiers above the water.

The name of Blois alone calls to mind a whole century of history, brilliant and troubled in turn, like the reign of the Valois kings. It was a period of marvelous festivals and tragedies. The château, which was the theater of important historical events, illustrates the evolution of French architecture from the fifteenth to the seventeenth century. One finds it immense and luxurious, occupying a natural site where it crowns the city. Blois is the most picturesque and charming city of the region. From the square in front of the château it spreads the pointed roofs of its houses and the spires of its churches out over the hillside as it slopes down to the river. The closely woven fabric formed by its roofs gives an inkling of the tangle of narrow streets and old quarters that follow the contours of the rough terrain. When you enter this maze, how many surprises and discoveries await you! It is rare today to find a city almost intact since the sixteenth century and whose original character has been preserved in spite of the opening of many streets during the last century.

The city has many buildings, all of which are remarkable. Among the most famous is Anne of Brittany's little house which stood formerly in the middle of wonderful gardens laid out during the reign of Louis XII. In town, beside half-timbered houses with sculpted ornaments are a few Renaissance mansions. Their names are Alluye, Sardini and Belot, and they were built by courtiers, financiers and nobles who revolved around the king. You can only discover the city on foot, for you must often go up or down a few steps, take a narrow passage or a steep alley. Sometimes a door standing ajar is an invitation: behind it is hidden a pretty paved courtyard with a gallery, a staircase with banisters or a turret with a sculpted door. Of the city's many churches only two remain: the Gothic cathedral dedicated to St. Louis and the very beautiful St. Nicholas's church, which is partly Romanesque.

But the château is certainly the masterpeice of the city. It overlooks Blois from a rocky spur which can be seen from very far away. At first sight it is a strange edifice made up of four or five castles, built successively on the site of an ancient fortress. Of these structures built at different times, three can still be seen: the château built by Louis XII, the Francis I wing and the Gaston d'Orléans wing. Their very dissimilar façades unite curiously to constitute the edifice we see today: a juxtaposition of three projects that are completely different in structure and decorative system.

One arrives on the square opposite the Louis XII wing which is of totally Gothic conception. The polychromy of the brick and stone walls gives the façades a note of discreet gaiety, the expression of flowery and anecdotal late Gothic art. The courtyard façade of the Francis I wing seems by contrast more composed and of a dazzling whiteness with decoration in very low relief. This part is entirely inspired by the Italian example, as is illustrated by the magnificent projecting staircase which harmoniously associates a Gothic structure with the themes of the Italianized decoration. This building's other façade which formerly opened onto the gardens, is more resolutely Italian. In the walls are open loggias in clumsy imitation of those of Bramante at the Vatican.

Closing the courtyard, around the corner from the Francis I wing, is the building raised by Gaston d'Orléans, which remains unfinished. The king's brother, who was fascinated by architecture, dreamed of building a classical palace, Versailles before the letter. His project was carried out only in part, due to a lack of money, and the previous structures were preserved. During the usual visits, this part of the castle is often ignored, to the benefit of the two others. For the average tourist, Blois is above all the assassination of the Guises and Catherine de' Medici's poison closets. But let's leave these curiosities to sensation lovers and stop a while in front of Gaston d'Orléans work. This wing differs from the two others by its majesty and balance. Each detail of the decoration contributes to this strict composition with its rhythmic façades. A

whole century of research was necessary to attain this classical perfection which was to be imitated at Versailles and in all the Ile-de-France. The inner courtyard of the château of Blois gives a view of the stages through which the still Gothic, late fifteenth-century French architecture was to pass as it experienced the marvelous adventure of the Renaissance and arrived at the strictness of classicism.

On the road out of Blois, lost in the forest of Melineuf, stands the Renaissance château of Bury. In the sixteenth century, at about two kilometers (roughly, one mile) from the château of Blois and in exact prolongation of it, a lane led through the forest to Bury, six miles away. Today only ruins are left of Bury, for in the seventeenth century it was razed stone by stone. Built by Florimond Robertet between 1514 and 1524, it marked one of the first appearances of Italianism in France. Seventeenth century drawings show that it set a fashion in the Vale of the Loire as much by its decoration which was of tramontane inspiration as by the regular disposition of its façades and the choice of its plan. One could talk for a long time about a problem that is properly the domain of architectural experts, but one is above all moved at the sight of such neglect. A tower whose walls are cracked through and through emerges from very dense vegetation, and you see part of the supporting wall of a gallery overrun by brambles. Here and there in the grass you stump your foot against a stone or a fragment of sculpture. Iconography allows us to reconstitute the buildings fairly accurately and you find yourself dreaming of an imaginary castle in the heart of a wooded spot that has been prepared to receive this sumptuous residence.

As you leave Bury, the valley of the Cisse descends toward the Loire delivering up, as it meanders, the rustic church of St. Segondin and the ruins of the abbey of Guiche, which was the lodging place in the thirteenth century of the recluses of St. Claire.

Here you return to the right bank of the Loire, just beyond Blois, and enter Touraine, but the separation of the two provinces cannot be seen in the landscape. The hills are just slightly higher and are covered in places with vineyards while the limestone walls of tufa begin to appear, dotted with habitations of cave-dwellers.

At the outposts of Touraine, on the high left bank, Chaumont castle rears its big round towers above the Loire. Seen from so far away, it has a lordly air and would make you think of some impregnable fortress if the façades did not have broad windows let into them and the watchpaths were not decorated with bas-reliefs, the tower now being only the prerogative of feudal power. The inner courtyard, with its staircase decorated with Renaissance motifs, is that of a pleasure palace, being open since the eighteenth century on a view of the Valley.

The Touraine

Custom has it that Amboise is the first city of Touraine. Built at the junction of the Loire and the valley of the Amasse which create the rocky spur on which the castle stands, Amboise is the typical city of the banks of the Loire. It is reflected in the waters of the river whose course is divided by a shady island.

In this broad and peaceful landscape the château occupies a strategic position at one end of the plateau. Above a massive rampart, the Renaissance façades contrast by their refinement. At a glance you take in this curious superposition: rampart, open gallery, balcony and dormer windows. One senses here a grandiose plan of which only a part remains: young Charles VIII wanted to make his native château into a palace worthy of Italy, which had enchanted him. Of the vast group of buildings that occupied the whole spur in the fifteenth century, there remain only the two towers, Hurtault and Minimes, the king's quarters and St. Hubert's chapel. In spite of the unfortunate restorations of the last century, one can appreciate the innovations introduced when this residence was built. A certain studied elegance can already be seen in the entrance hall of Hurtault Tower, with the sculpted panel bearing the coats-of-arms of France and Brittany, and on the outer façade of the living quarters where the buttresses embellished with niches, the fretwork balustrade and the dormer windows bristling with pinnacles compose an ensemble unprecedented in the mansions of the Vale of the Loire. In spite of the desire for novelty and the richness of the decoration, the château is relatively unmarked by the new art from Italy, and St. Hubert's chapel, the work of a Flemish master, is faithful to the purest flamboyant Gothic tradition.

The city holds happy surprises: a Renaissance city hall, a belfry-gate, and outside the walls the beautiful St. Denis's church built in the twelfth century in a Romanesque style very much influenced by Angevin art: segmental and finely ribbed vaults. Behind the château the Vale of the Amasse leads to Clos-Lucé, a little manor-house of brick and stone where Leonardo da Vinci lived during his last years. Toward the south jutting above the woods, a curious pagoda stands where the lanes cross, reminding you of the pomp of Chanteloup castle, built by the Duke of Choiseul.

As it approaches Tours, the Loire Valley broadens as far as the banks of the Cher, forming a vast panorama. By their variety and richness, the plants growing on the hillsides justify by themselves the name of "garden of France". In this region of fruit trees and vineyards, on sunny terraces you will also see the palm tree, the eucalyptus, the orange tree and the holm oak. The variety of plants in the Loire region contrasts with that of the plateau, which is less rich and less well-known. It has hidden treasures, however, along the roads skirting the secondary valleys.

At Rochecorbon, a little stream which we have already seen in the Blesois rejoins the Loire: it is the Cisse, which from Vouvray to Vernou flows through one of the most famous wine districts of the region. Its deep, narrow valley and an infinity of vales and glens are the heart of a Touraine too little known to outsiders. A detour at the place called "Vaufouinard" will lead you to a little castle. Lost in the depths of an immense and somewhat neglected wooded park, Jallanges is not easily reached. After having crossed a mossy lane, then two courtyards bordered with outbuildings, one discovers a building of the late fifteenth century in brick with stone cornerstones. The façade has broad mullioned windows let in it and is topped with high dormer windows whose pointed gables stand out against a slate roof. In the center, a small polygonal tower, crowned by an overhanging top floor, houses the spiral staircase that leads to the second floor and attic. The entire façade is decorated with a great number of sculptured motifs in the flowery style of late Gothic: an ogee arch with a terminal fleuron above the front door and sculpted ornaments holding the window moldings. The quality and variety of this amazing decoration are astonishing in this forgotten spot.

North of Jallanges, the manor-houses of La Côte, Valmer and La Vallière await the curious visitor who goes astray on a little road or who arrives by way of the river from downstream. Descending the valley of the Brenne you arrive at the gates of Tours, after a stop at the fortified farm of Meslay whose front gate and colossal tithing-barn call to mind the former wealth of the powerful abbey of Marmoutier. That important monastic center stands not far away on the right bank of the Loire. Of this group of buildings, founded by St. Martin, there remains only a very small part which escaped the demolition that took place at the beginning of the mineteenth century: the fortified gate of the Crosse, the chapel of the Seven Sleepers and the Tower of the Bells, as well as fragments of the outer wall. Recent digging has unearthed the foundations of a Gothic church which is said to have been the model for the cathedral of Tours.

Coming from Marmoutier, you see the capital of Touraine rise behind the island-strewn Loire: "Tours, like Venice, seems to emerge from the waters"; but today it is more difficult to see what Balzac was referring to.

Although the changes brought about during past centuries and the bombardments of the last war have changed its appearance, the city of Tours is modern only on the surface. As soon as you leave the large central axis, fragments of the old city can be seen. A few restored blocks of the old quarter are a quite faithful reconstitution of the medieval city, such as Plumereau Square and Change Street. And you should wander through streets still untouched by restoration and whose names call to mind the daily life of former times: Broom Street, Crossbow Street and Three Desks Street.

The ancient Gallo-roman city of the Turones was encircled by an outer wall that is still to be seen enclosing the square where the amphitheater was situated and on which the first St. Gatien's cathedral was built. The religious metropolis, which counted sixty buildings in the late fifteenth century, has certainly lost some of its power but a few churches remain: St. Gatien, whose construction lasted from the thirteenth to the sixteenth century, is the most beautiful of the group, and the little cloister of Psalette, next to it, is a delicate work of the early Renaissance.

The former abbey of St. Julian, once very vast, is reduced to a Gothic church with a Romanesque belfry-porch and very thoroughly remodelled monastic buildings. But it is St. Martin's collegiate church, a famous place of pilgrimage during the Middle Ages, which has suffered most from destruction and indifference. All that remains today are two stately towers and some scattered vestiges in the neighborhood. Among these, a cloister dating from the early Renaissance evokes by its lavish sculpture the splendor of the art of the Loire region. The first great period of secular constructions is situated in the fifteenth and sixteenth centuries when Tours was a royal city. The city's prosperity was seen in the new structures: houses and private mansions built by rich merchants turned financiers to the king. The last war destroyed these buildings in part; those remaining are often very much restored. Of the Beaune-Semblençay mansion there remains only a gallery wall and a fountain. After the bombardments, only the façade of the Goüin mansion was left and it had to be rebuilt stone by stone. Sometimes, walking at random through the streets, one sees a few mansions: Binet, Robin-Quantin, Babou de la Bourdaisière and the curious brick house wrongly called "Tristan". These houses, which were built by rich burgers, were of stone, while the more democratic heart of the medieval city was built of brick and wood. Tours was at this period a flourishing city and an artistic captial: painters, sculptors, tapestry-makers and glassmakers, natives of the region or professionals attracted by the presence of the king, produced their best works here.

The second period of construction is situated around the eighteenth century when the "stone bridge" was built and the great north-south opening was effected which completely changed the appearance of the medieval city. But it is the mansions of the seventeenth and eighteenth centuries that have most suffered from the bombardments of the last war and then from the reconstruction. The Mame mansion is now one of the rare examples of classical architecture in Tours.

A short distance from the city, between the Loire and the Cher, a little house of brick and stone flanked by a small tower is all that remains of the Plessis-lès-Tours castle. As soon as he was crowned, Louis XI showed his preference for this residence which was more a country house than a sinister fortified castle born of the romantic imagination of Sir Walter Scott. Nearby on the banks of the Loire, the priory of St. Cosmas, now restored, stands beside the ruins of one of the region's oldest

Romanesque churches. The fifteenth-century priory quarters call to mind the last years of Ronsard who is buried in this garden of roses and box-trees.

On the opposite bank, facing St. Cosmas, St. Cyr hill rises above the Loire. The steepness of the cliff is masked by the abundant vegetation, a natural setting of greenery, dotted with villas and country houses. One of them is Grenadière where Balzac sometimes stayed.

After Tours, the right bank of the river is marked by an impressive number of châteaux and manor-houses as far as the junction with the Vienne. On Fondettes hill the manor-house of Chatigny, which can be seen from the levee, is a simple late fifteenth-century structure of checkered brick and stone. The polychromy of its materials is current in the Loire Valley, especially between Luynes and Fondettes, and even modest houses use this this technique on the upper floors, chimneys and gables. This decoration is sometimes used along with ornaments of the early Renaissance, as in Vieilles Ligneries manor-house. Near the lush green valley of the Choisille, this pretty sixteenth century building protects its solitude, far from curious visitors. How could you imagine that behind this unpretentious farm is hidden the "country house" of a hunamistic man of the Church?

On the right bank of the Loire between Chatigny and Luynes, the tufa cliff is perforated with cave dwellings as far as Luyne castle, which is built on a rocky spur. It is a stern fortress which commands from the top of its eight towers the Valley road and access to the plateau and which served as a look-out post to detect invaders coming from the river. Another witness to a warlike past is Cinq-Mars-la-Pile. You can still see in the park, among the filled-in moats which have been turned into gardens, two towers razed to the "height of infamy" on Richelieu's orders. It is well known that brilliant young Cinq-Mars, the friend of Louis XIII, was himself beheaded for treachery.

Between Cinq-Mars-la-Pile and Langeais, the road follows the Loire, which spreads out here in all its splendor, swollen by the waters of the Cher. It now attains its full volume, flowing abundantly and stretching out many arms to embrace islands covered with thick pastureland and water-willow beds. Langeais castle, situated in the center of the town, seems the very image of the medieval castle of our childhood history books: a massive fortress with bare walls topped with machicolations and a watchpath, and whose thick towers defend it from all aggressions. The addition, in the nineteenth century, of a rather fantastic drawbridge, adds to the illusion. Built by Louis XI, this castle should have been one of those bastions that militarily bolt in a province. Unfinished because useless and inefficient after the progress made in artillery, it is one of the last great fortresses.

Not far from Langeais, to the north, is a Renaissance château which is deserted and forgotten by all and whose existence is not even suspected by most Touraine people

because it is not easy to get to: of Hommes, hidden in the bend of a lane near a farm, there remain today only ruins surrounded by running water. An inobservant passerby will hardly see it, overgrown as it is by vegetation, brambles, ivy and vines climbing over the stones. A wormeaten door leads to the inner courtyard. Although the château is completely ruined, one may find under the Virginia creeper some sculpted foliage, a scallop shell or the capital of a column worthy of Azay-le-Rideau. The arcades of an open gallery are assaulted by vines and elder branches. What was the fate of this buiding, the causes of its ruin? All these questions remain unanswered for its history is unknown to us.

You will return to the Loire after Langeais, opposite Bréhémont where river shad and salmon fishers still drop their nets. Here time flows smoothly and a last ray of sunlight lingers on the still boats in the evening splendor. This landscape of great delicacy is one of the most beautiful in Touraine.

The Touraine of the Old Regime ended at Langeais. Today its territory extends to the Bourgueil wine district and its environs. The Loire levee, from Langeais to Bourgueil, is edged below with an uninterrupted row of dazzlingly white houses. Sheepmen's houses, vine-growers' small-holdings, market gardens, all are carefully built of this beautiful building stone which becomes slightly pink in the sun. On the vine-covered slopes of the softly rounded hillocks, the château of Benais can be seen behind the trees; rebuilt in the last century, it retains from the former edifice a Renaissance entrance pavilion.

The village of Restigné has a few outstanding houses, symbols of the wine district's affluence and pleasant way of life. At its center, Bourgueil has kept the memory of a celebrated Benedictine abbey and still owns a parish church with beautiful Angevin vaults.

At the next stop we shall visit the little château of Réaux which was built in the early sixteenth century by a member of a great Touraine family, the Briçonnets. This Renaissance structure is in reality only a small castle whose walls are entirely made of brick and stone. But here the materials alternate imaginatively and humorously in different designs: checkerboards, zigzags and herringbones. It is an unexpected decorative minglement.

Touraine ends at Réaux, but the landscape on the banks of the Loire hardly changes until Saumur: there are few outstanding buildings except for a series of white houses built along the levee.

The Anjou

To enter the Vale of Anjou it is preferable to take the left bank, crossing the Loire at Port-Boulet, in order to arrive a little to its west at its junction with the Vienne at Candes-Saint-Martin. The countryside is more varied and picturesque and many edifices catch your attention.

The village of Candes calls to mind St. Martin who often retired to this hermitage. The curious fortified twelfth-century church, built on the site of the saint's cell, is worth a visit. The porch opening onto the Loire is surprising and the massive bare wall is enlivened by small columns and statues which unite Romanesque austerity to fine Angevin-style decoration. This elegance is found again inside the church where a delicate monolithic column holds the ribs of highly segmented vaults. The village, whose ancient houses hang from the hillside and gather around the church and a little turreted castle, overlooks the vast panoramam of the junction of the Loire and the Vienne.

Between Candes and Montsoreau, the narrow road running along the Loire is bordered with buildings that are for the most part very old and bear witness to the past wealth of the region. Montsoreau, situated between the hill and the river that formerly washed its walls, presents its façade to the sun. In spite of the watchpath with machicolations, no sign of austerity can be seen on its golden stone walls. Curious two-storeyed dormer windows decorated with pinnacles and crockets let light into the high attic. The inner façade is embellished with a staircase tower decorated with a strange bas-relief: above a recumbent deer, two monkeys hold a cask of wine and a banner with the lord's motto: "I will do it."

The road that follows the Loire from Montsoreau to Saumur has shady banks overlooked by a steep hill. Above a crag a village is half-hidden in the greenery, a church timidly points its steeple, a manor-

56

house is hiding. The unpretentious church of Parnay clings to the top of the cliff, while Souzay manor, a little fifteenth-century structure, leans its crenelated towers against the rock.

The abbey of Fontevraud is very close. Founded in the early twelfth century by Robert d'Arbrissel, it united two distinct communities of men and women under the direction of an abbess. The role played by the abbey in the monastic life of the medieval Western world explains the great size of its buildings. The abbatial church is no doubt, since the ruin of the collegiate church of St. Martin of Tours, the region's masterpiece of Romanesque architecture. The nave, which is covered with a very finely proportioned vault, is related to the Romanesque tradition of southwestern France. In the transept one discovers a fine example of medieval statuary: recumbent statues on the tombs of the Plantagenets who made Fontevraud their necropolis.

Leaving Fontevraud one returns to the Loire by a winding path: the valley of the Thouet, on the Touraine-Anjou border, is a perfect setting for a romantic walk. The course of this little stream continues, tortuous and narrow, to Saumur, crossing a countryside thickly dotted with manor-houses.

At Montreuil-Bellay the river encloses the steep hill bearing the castle that is formed of a disorderly group of walls, ruins and disparate structures. Built in the fifteenth century, it is composed of four blocks of living quarters with staircase turrets, a haphazard juxtaposition which

the visitor finds charming because it evokes the traditional feudal residence. The road running along the Thouet leads to Saumur, which, like Blois, should be viewed from the opposite bank of the Loire. The fifteenth-century town hall on the riverbank which is flanked by watch turrets, and the sharp steeple of St. Peter's church capture our attention less than the enormous mass of the castle overlooking the city. Situated on a hilltop, it occupies a place comparable to that of Amboise. Its high white façades and towers with pointed roofs call to mind the celebrated miniatures of the *Very Rich Hours of the Duke of Berry*. Unfortunately, the decoration of the dormer windows and the delicate superstructures that embellished the upper floors and the roof have disappeared. Today we must try hard to imagine the country house dear to King René.

In town another house, the mansion of the Queen of Sicily, with its beautiful flamboyant dormer windows, was built by King René's mother, Yolanda of Aragon. Nearby, there are few structures on the right bank except for Boumois castle, built on the bank of the Authion whose course here is parallel to that of the Loire. Partly rebuilt in the fifteenth century, it appears from behind a leafy lane. The buildings are disposed simply ; the main body of the building overlooks two lower wings. A water-filled moat surrounds it on all sides. Like Amboise, it is a castle whose rich flamboyant decoration illustrates the short moment when Italianism had not yet come to France.

For us to reach Angers, the left bank is much more charming because of its landscape and its buildings.

At Trèves a colossal keep thirty meters (100 feet) high juts out over the Loire. Cunault, the neighboring village, is celebrated for its beautiful Romanesque church, the younger sister of Vézelay and St. Benedict's. Its construction took place from the eleventh to the thirteenth century. You can appreciate the tall, graceful proportions of the building and the depth of the nave, accentuated as it is by the shortening of the central hall. The indirect lighting which comes from the narrow openings of the side aisles, softly shapes the volumes and gives them an amazing fullness.

The surrounding countryside permits us to make other discoveries: the Romanesque church of St. Cosmas's priory and the outbuildings of Pimpéan castle. In the Valley of the Layon is one of the most beautiful castles of the region, Brissac. Its curious façade appears incoherent, the unfinished reconstruction showing the contributions of successive owners. Two great towers with machicolations, the vestiges of a fifteenth-century castle, frame a great seventeenth-century entrance pavilion decorated with bossing. But unity is maintained by the use of the same materials: schist for the walls and building stone for the ties. Inside is a monumental majestic staircase, one of the noblest in France.

To the south, in the direction of Cholet, Basse-Guerche and Lavouer are typically Angevin manor-houses. As at Brissac schist replaces tufa, which is reserved for the corner stones and window and door frames. With the change of material begins the passage to another region: to the south, the region of Mauges, land of the Chouans, announces the Vendée. We see the Loire again at Ponts-de-Cé, near a castle built by King René. All that remains of it is a keep crowned by a watchpath.

Then from Rochefort to Chalonnes the twisting road rises, crossing the vineyards in terraces above the Loire. Opposite the junction with the Layon, on the right bank, the "coulee of Serrant" shelters the castle of the same name. Less grandiose than Brissac, it unites harmoniously a Renaissance structure with classical decoration. In the middle of a large romantic park a beautiful pond holds up a mirror of water to the façcades.

On the same bank, to the west, a ruined tower, traditionally attributed to Gilles de Rais, seems balanced on a schist crag like a bastion turned toward Britanny. This will be our last stop in the Vale of the Loire. Beyond, another country begins. This is the road to the sea, made detectable by a slight nuance of light and by the rising wind. The landscape is harsher, the Vale narrows and the Loire now flows between high granite walls.

And yet, on the left bank, two small buildings call to mind the Angevin gentleness sung by the poet. At Liré, the native region of Joachim du Bellay, stands the chapel of Bourgonnière: this jewel of the

Renaissance is like a goodbye to the Loire Valley.

We couldn't leave Anjou, however, without stopping in its capital. Angers is the only city built away from the river. Contrary to Blois and Tours it does not occupy a site that can be taken in at a glance. The castle's mass and that of the cathedral on the edge of the hill hide the old city.

This castle, a formidable fortress built by St. Louis, would appear more imposing if its towers had not been lowered. Inside, the "châtelet" or "little castle" is in fact a country house which calls to mind the memory of King René. St. Maurice's cathedral is the most original Gothic church in France: its single nave is covered with a high-pitched vault, halfway between the traditional pointed vaults and cupolas, a striking testimony of the Angevin Gothic style. It formerly contained the celebrated Apocalypse tapestries which are now in the castle. It is well known that they were made in the fourteenth century for Louis I of Anjou by Nicolas Bataille according to drawings by Hennequin of Bruges.

Several famous churches and abbeys remain around the cathedral. The choir of St. Sergius's church is a masterpiece of the Angevin Gothic style. St. Aubin's abbey has kept only its cloister, now situated inside the perimeter walls of the prefecture. Its arcades are decorated with painted scenes; the finesse and precision of the design are in keeping with the freshness of the colors. In the quarter beyond the Maine, St. John's hospital, a vast medieval block that has been transformed into a museum, houses tapestries by Lurçat. Ronceray abbey close by is also an interesting example of Angevin art.

Angers is one of those provincial capitals that remain pleasant towns but can be understood only from the inside. Like those of Bourges and Blois, Angers's old quarter is quite homogenous and well-integrated into the framework of daily life and has not been excessively restored. Fine fifteenth- and sixteenth-century houses line the streets where you still see old signs: Adam's house and the one of the beautiful Angevin woman, the Pincé mansion and the Barrault house. On the other side of the Maine, the former home of the Penitents surprises you by the refinement of its Renaissance decoration which is quite unexpected in such a building. But at Angers, the main part of the old quarters is made up of seventeenth- and eighteenth-century mansions which bear witness to the city's prosperity at the end of the Old Regime.

Angers is situated a little back from the Vale of the Loire at the junction of three streams which meet in a single arm, the Maine. The streams, the Sarthe, the Mayenne and the Loir, all flow through wooded districts before meeting. Lush green meadows make of the region surrounding Angers a land of incomparable freshness, dotted with many castles. We shall give no itinerary here, for the pleasure of discovery results from a certain imagination being exercised as you walk along.

A few castles should be seen for their typically regional character or for their architectural interest. Northeast of Angers, here is Plessis-Macé, on the bank of the Mayenne. In the late fifteenth century, on the site of a former fortress were built elegant structures crowned with pronouncedly overhanging upper floors. The whimsical plan of the building is not lacking in charm, and the variations in level of the roofs, the jagged silhouette of the steep gables and the high dormer windows accentuate its medieval aspect. In the main courtyard St. Michael's chapel has retained its gallery with open-work from the flamboyant period, a rare and precious model of late fifteenth-century wooden architecture.

The lover of architecture cannot be unaware of Plessis-Bourré castle on the banks of the Sarthe. It is one of the most important and best-preserved buildings in France from the second half of the fifteenth century. Built by Jean Bourré at the same time as Langeais, it was finished in 1473. Although still feudal in conception, with its broad moat and its defensive apparatus, the plan of the buildings announces a new day. The lower perimeter wall allows one to see the seigniorial living quarters situated at the back of the courtyard and opening widely onto the outside world; on the side, an open gallery links the chapel to the main part of the building. In opposition to Langeais, which is still rooted in feudal tradition, Plessis-Bourré affirms a new concept of the nobleman's residence; the disposition of the building, which was revolutionary at the time, was to exert a great influence on constructions in the Vale of the Loire during the sixteenth century.

Before we leave Anjou, a last walk will lead us to Montgeoffroy, east of Angers. This château, of great simplicity, unrolls its long, white façade at the end of a lane. Field Marshal de Contades built it in the 1750s. The apartments contain a unique set of eighteenth-century furniture, which has never been dispersed, a circumstance rare in France. The chapel prolonging the right wing belonged to the earlier sixteenth-century structure. The gate with its pointed arch, a beautiful octagonal bell-tower and especially a superb Renaissance stained glass window do not belie its reputation as Anjou's most handome seigniorial chapel.

Compared to Touraine and to the Blesois, Anjou is no doubt less rich in great castles, having ten at the most. But if one lingers here, one finds a countryside rich in beautiful residences which are more familial than princely. They express with grace, poetry and tenderness the soul of the region.

vallée de la loire

valley of the loire
Tal der Loire

1. orléanais

7/8 . Saint-Benoît.
9 . Germigny-des-Prés.

◄ 6 . La Sange.

10 . Orléans.
11 . Jargeau.

12/13 . Beaugency.
14 . Meung-sur-Loire.

15 . Sully-sur-Loire.

2. blésois

16 . Ménars.

17 . Ménars.
18 . Talcy.
19 . Talcy.

24 . Chambord.

25 . Chambord.

26/27 . Chambord.

28/29 . Chambord.

Chambord . 30 ▶

31 . Chambord.

32 . Villesavin.
33 . Beauregard.

34 . Beauregard.

Blois . 35 ▶

36/37 . Blois.

38/39/40 . Blois.

41/42 . Blois.

43 . Blois.

44 . Chaumont-sur-Loire.
45/46 . La Cisse à Cangey.

47/48/49 . Chaumont-sur-Loire.

Chaumont-sur-Loire . 50 ▶

3. touraine

51 . Touraine.

52 . Pagode de Chanteloup.
53/54/55 . Clos-Lucé.

56/57/58 . Amboise.

59/60 . Amboise.

61 . Amboise.

62 . Bagneux.
63 . Plessis-lès-Tours.
64 . Prieuré de Saint-Cosme.

65/66 . Tours.

AU BON VIN DE TOURAINE

67 . Rochecorbon.
68 . Vouvray.
69 . Azay-le-Rideau.

Vouvray . 70 ▶

71 . Luynes.
72 . Gizeux.

73 . Les Réaux.
74/75 . Langeais.

76 . Langeais.

4. anjou

77 . Candes-Saint-Martin.

78 . Montreuil-Bellay.
79/80 . Montsoreau.

81 . Candes-Saint-Martin.
82 . Cunault.
83 . Fontevraud.

84 / 85 / 86 / 87 . Saumur.

Serrant . 88 ▶

89 . Brissac.

90 . Brissac.
91 . Serrant.

92/93
94/95 . Angers.

96 . Angers.

97
98/99 . Plessis-Bourré
100 . Plessis-Macé.

Orbières . 101 ▶

The Cher Valley

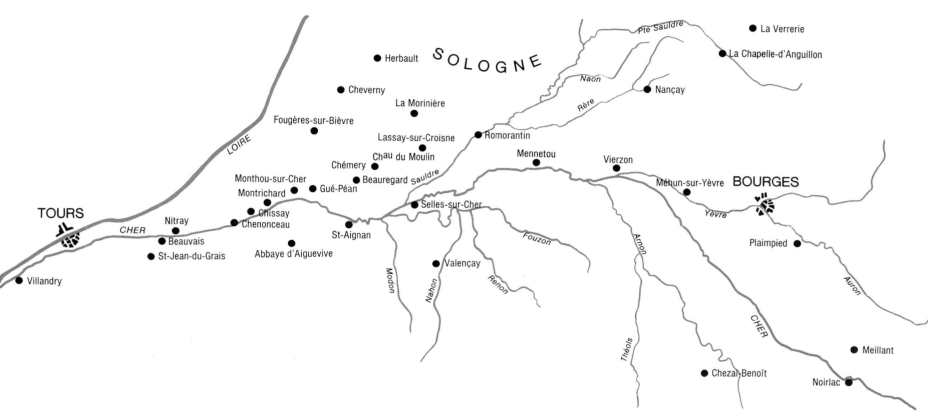

Before approaching the Cher Valley in its lower region, we must not forget Bourges and Upper Berry which have a particular place in the "Art of the Loire". Like Tours and Blois, Bourges has benefitted from circumstances favorable to its artistic flowering. In the fourteenth century the duchy was detached from the crown and became the domain of Jean de Berry who made of Bourges an artistic center unique in France. Later Charles VII inherited his property. Bourges then became the point of departure for the conquest of the English-occupied kingdom. Installed in the castle of Mehun-on-Yèvre, nearby, the king received the financial support of Jacques Cœur, the richest man in the kingdom. In the late Middle Ages Bourges became an economic and intellectual center, attracting and holding great fortunes and artists. To these historic factors is added the particular geographical position of this border region between the north and the south of France, favorable to all kinds of exchange. From the medieval period Bourges has kept a splendid cathedral, one of the finest examples of French Gothic architecture. Its unique plan is not lacking in originality: the double side aisles of decreasing height allow the openings to be arranged in tiers and permit a distribution of the light that transforms the building into a real greenhouse. An exceptional set of thirteenth- to sixteenth-century stained glass windows accentuates the wonder one feels and creates, by the variety of colors, a light that is completely unreal.

The late fifteenth and early sixteenth centuries have left, in the field of secular architecture, many examples of the prosperity and wealth of the town. The best known is, of course, the mansion built by Charles VII's financier, the unfortunate Jacques Cœur. And yet a few Renaissance residences, like the Cujas mansion and especially the Lallemand mansion, are, by the refinement of their sculpted decoration, the equals of their Touraine and Blesois counterparts.

In general, the old city has kept its integrity, more even than Blois. Established on a hillside overlooked by the cathedral, half-timbered houses alternate there with handsome mansions set in gardens.

In the immediate environs of the city, one finds a great many buildings worthy of attention, churches, castles and abbeys, among which it is difficult to choose. Romanesque art is particularly well represented in Berry, with the celebrated abbeys of Noirlac and Chezal-Benoît and several churches that are more modest but have abundant sculpted decorations, like those of Plaimpied and Germigny-l'Exempt. The castles of Berry long remained faithful to the Gothic tradition, as they embellished their inner walls with luxurious and flowery decorations, of which the finest example is probably Meillant.

Northeast of Bourges, between the Loire and the Sauldre, several small castles, most of them unknown, are worth mentioning: Boucard, Blancafort, Pezeau and Buranlure, with their musical names. If I had to select one it would be Verrerie, a few miles from La-Chapelle-d'Angillon, the country of "*grand* Meaulnes". It is situated in a forest, facing an immense pond, on the melancholy site that inspired Alain Fournier. Built in the early sixteenth century of brick and stone, it unites the delicate colors of the materials with the refinement of the sculpted decorations. Precious in appearance, it seems like a product of Italy in the middle of stern Berry. Not far from there, Aubigny-sur-Nère, a one-street village, situated on the border of Sologne, surprises us by a series of half-timbered houses. The care given to these structures as well as a recent restoration give this country village a peculiar appearance which makes it seem to have come out of a Grimm's fairy tale.

At Vierzon, the Cher begins its lower course and leaves Berry to skirt the south of the Blois region before entering Touraine. Still choppy in Berry, it becomes calmer near the Loire. Its broad valley bordered with low hills is not very picturesque but it is nonetheless not monotonous. The market gardens and the meadows are broken up by rows of alders and poplars which are filled with birds on sunny days. The horizon is limited on either side by gentle slopes covered with vineyards.

The passage from Berry to the Blesois occurs after the fortified village of

Mennetou at Selles-on-Cher, formerly known as Selles-in-Berry. The town has two castles on the same site: the first one, of the fourteenth century, replaced a former fortress; the second, which is unfinished, was built in the seventeenth century by Philippe de Béthune, Sully's brother. Opposite its entrance, the Romanesque church possesses the singularity of a double sculpted frieze which ornaments the entire apse wall.

At Romorantin the Cher welcomes the Sauldre, a slow, lazy stream from Sologne which is broken up by ponds. It was here that Francis I spent his childhood and planned to build his dream palace, before deciding on Chambord. The Sauldre demarcates, together with the Beuvron, a little wooded region which effects the transition from Sologne to the Blois region, where the density of castles is great. The largest and best known is Cheverny, a huge residence of the seventeenth century, which is situated in a park with magnificent foliage. Cheverny is one of the rare Loire castles that still belongs to a descendant of the family that owned it in the sixteenth century: Hurault de Vibraye de Cheverny.

The structure we see today was built in 1634 on the site of a sixteenth-century manor-house. it is composed of a high and narrow central rectangular block flanked by two square pavilions with lantern-turrets on their roofs. The interest of Cheverny lies also in the interior decoration of Louis XIII period panelling with paintings representing Don Quixote's life and with Gobelin tapestries.

More modest, but equally attractive, are the manor-houses of Chémery, Herbault, Moulin and Morinière. The castle of Moulin, built on a terrace surrounded by broad ditches, has brick and stone façades ornamented with a black lozenge design. This rustic decoration, which is common in Sologne, is in no way inconsistent with a military apparatus that became useless in the late fifteenth century.

More recent, but having the same character, its neighbor, La Morinière, presents to the sun its pink brick walls and towers reflected by the stagnant waters of a pond. In the heart of a village, Fougères, a stocky fortress, seems to have been placed there on the square since its moat was filled in. An agreeable inner courtyard embellished by an open gallery and a staircase tower belies the harsh appearance of its outer wall.

Turning again toward the south we rejoin the Cher at Saint-Aignan; on the slopes this little town is overlooked by the château which was rebuilt in the sixteenth century. One arrives at the château from the Romanesque church by way of a stairway of 144 steps. The inner courtyard is closed on two sides by an L-shaped block of living quarters whose façades are adorned with superposed pilasters and dormer windows surmounted by high pediments. The other two sides of the terrace are bordered by a balustrade and open on a vast view of the valley. Near Saint-Aignan, on the left bank of the Cher, curious visitors will find the path leading to the ruins of Aiguevive Abbey.

Unconditional lovers of old stones are now trying to preserve these vestiges. But time is at work here and the building continues to deteriorate. In places, one can just barely see the outline of a fresco which will soon vanish completely. Between Saint-Aignan and Montrichard, the Cher takes in a stream with the amusing name of "Traine-Feuilles" (Drag-Leaves). It has its source in a forest surrounding Gué-Péan castle. At a bend in the lane one suddenly comes upon the castle set upon a softly rolling meadow. It is a structure of the sixteenth and seventeenth centuries in white stone with a slightly grey cast, but which a sunbeam can turn to pink. A little bridge astride a dry moat leads to the entrance gate flanked by truncated towers. The L-shaped living quarters, framed by two thick cylindrical towers, open onto a paved courtyard. In spite of the successive stages of constructions, Gué-Péan has kept a certain unity because of the beauty and luminosity of the stone. Without frills or any imposing feature, it is a charming place.

Following the course of the Cher, here we are at Montrichard, a medieval town built on the side of a chalky hill and crowned by a formidable square keep which rises in the midst of a pile of ruined ramparts and fortifications. To arrive there, you must climb to the upper city, which is constituted of semi-troglodytic habitations, paths, stairways and tiny hanging gardens. From there, you overlook a beautiful landscape and in one glimpse you take in the Cher Valley as far as

Touraine, as far as Chenonceau.

The road runs along the Cher at the foot of a cliff against which Chissay castle leans. Its Gothic façades, although very much remodelled, gracefully stand out against a cedar and plane-tree park.

Chenonceau owes its fame as much to its Renaissance architecture as to the originality of its location on the river. A long plane-tree avenue leads to the forecourt, then to the terrace, surrounded by a broad moat, on which still stands the keep of the Marques, the only primitive vestige. From the terrace, a few steps and a bridge lead to the château built in 1515 by Thomas Bohier on the piers of the former mill. It is a great square pavilion with turrets at the corners and whose façades date from the early Renaissance: openings framed by fluted pilasters, large dormer windows with pediments and candelabra. Inside, the straight staircase is the first of this style in the Loire Valley, along with the one at Bury castle, since destroyed.

The château, become the property of the crown, was given to Diane of Poitiers by Henry II. We owe to her the bridge over the Cher which was to connect the graceful residence of Thomas Bohier to the other bank.

Catherine de' Medici afterwards built the two floors of the gallery on the bridge. Its already classical and somewhat academic sobriety contrast with the highly refined decor of the Renaissance pavilion. This surprising structure was designed to astonish people and was the setting of lavish parties given by the sons of Catherine de' Medici. Besides the magnificence and the luxury of the building, one is struck today by the calm and serenity surrounding it. To feel the subtle charm of this alliance of stone and water, you must see Chenonceau in the winter or spring when its only ornament is the fog that rises from the river.

No large houses are to be seen between Chenonceau and Tours, but you may discover off the beaten track a few structures which are sometimes full of memories: Beauvais, which was built in the eighteenth century and was during the First Empire the setting for some "shady business". Its neighbor, Nitray, is a Renaissance manor-house whose gardens overlook the Cher. Each village that marks this road is richened by a church worthy of our interest or a forgotten building like the Romanesque priory of Saint-Jean-du-Grais.

Then the Cher flows along south of Tours and is completely canalized and broken up by reaches. It was still navigated here in the last century and a short canal connected it to the Loire, which it rejoins after having lazily crossed a sometimes flooded plain. Near the junction with the Loire Vilandry stands at the foot of a hill in the middle of a garden in the French style whose flower beds are arranged in terraces in the style of Renaissance gardens. The construction of the castle shows some analogies with Villesavin, for it is also the work of Jean Le Breton. The complete restorations it underwent in the eighteenth century and later have made it lose all its Renaissance character. It was, however, like Villesavin one of the first castles to break with medieval tradition, the corner towers being replaced by square pavilions. It is regrettable that since the gardens have been reconstructed, the romantic park, which as at Ussé and Azay constituted a setting of greenery, has disappeared.

From the terraces, one sees the junction of the two rivers whose "spit", which was built up in the eighteenth century, preserves the valley from catastrophical high waters. Calmed and canalized, the place of junction is a strange country where arms of stagnant water bordered by dense vegetation mingle with dikes and dead-end paths.

The Indre Valley

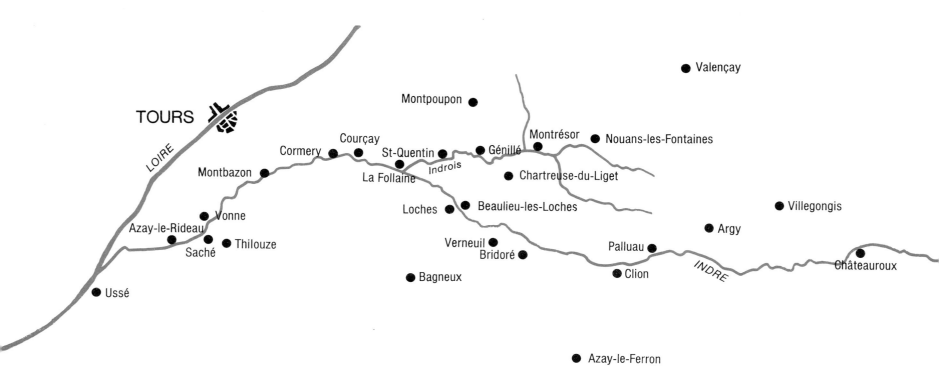

From the point of junction with the Cher the passage toward the Indre Valley is easy. The two rivers flow parallel to each other in the same vale. Contrary to the Cher, the Indre has no tributary. It is divided into a ramification of little arms separated by lines of poplars, willows and plane-trees.

On one of these arms stands Ussé opposite an immense valley which extends its alluvial plains beyond the Loire as far as the hill of Bourgueil. The castle is set at the base of a densely wooded, chalky cliff where it displays its white façades. The quality of the tufa gives the building an exceptional luminosity which is accentuated by the refinement of the decoration. More

than a defensive castle, it seems to be the survivor of a bygone time, harmoniously uniting the various stages of its construction and remodelling. In the seventeenth century the feudal aspect was somewhat attenuated by opening the courtyard onto the valley. A set of terraces today clears the view and permits us to see from quite a distance this beautiful front façade whose delicate Gothic ornamentation, veritable damascening in stone, stands out against the forest.

At a short distance, the most refined of the châteaux of the Loire is situated on an island in the Indre, whose waters reflect its façades. Azay-le-Rideau, built from 1518 to 1527 by G. Berthelot, has remained

166

unfinished: only two wings were built. The two blocks of living quarters, arranged in a right angle, open onto the main courtyard, which is flanked at the outer angles by corbelled towers which are crowned with false machicolations. It is the very type of the château of the Loire, with its feudal form and graceful Renaissance ornamentation.

The disposition of the façades demonstrates a set purpose of regularity which was obtained by the intersection of the super-imposed pilasters framing the openings and by the double set of moldings separating the floors. The decor remains reduced to the essentials, however, the pilasters, window rails and piers are bare and the sobriety of the walls brings out the preciosity of the sculpted features. They are of exceptional quality: capitals, dormer window pediments, foliage and especially the fine vertical section of the staircase forming a triumphal arch are set off by the simplicity of the walls. The Italian-type staircase is covered with coffered vaulting decorated with medallions. The balanced rhythm of the façades and the regular disposition of the structure demonstrate a sense of moderation rarely seen. It has often been said of Azay-le-Rideau that it is the most feminine of the châteaux of the Loire, because of its grace, its delicacy and the happy harmony which associates the beauty of its natural setting with the splendor of the edifice.

A pale imitation of Azay and probably of more recent construction, its neighbor, Islette, also stands on the banks of the

Indre. If it had not suffered deplorable defacement during the last century, one could detect many analogies between the two structures, especially in the sculpted decoration.

Upstream from Azay, the Indre becomes more secret and less easily approached than the Cher; it flows south of Tours in a more steep-sided valley and is often hidden behind a curtain of trees. It is choppy, sometimes rapid and broken by mills and dams, sometimes whimsical and slow, sprawling out in the middle of meadows in broad loops full of water lilies. Its banks, as well as the southerly plateau and secondary valleys, are a setting for many manor-houses and charming cottages, like that of Balzac at Saché and the manor-house of Vonnes, described by the writer under the name of Clochegourde in *The Lily in the Valley*.

The little castle *(châtelet)* of Thilouse surprises by its isolated situation in the middle of a field. Alone on the plateau, it is a small building composed of a square pavilion with four cylindrical towers at the corners. It stands on an island in the middle of a small pond which serves as a moat. The entrance through the northern façade is a semi-circular-arched door preceded by a fixed bridge which has replaced the drawbridge. Above the door, a pilastered window is surmounted by a dormer window whose pediment is decorated with a scallop shell. The surrounding garden, overrun with weeds and given over to brambles and underbrush, seems to be trying with its pitiful weapons to protect the mystery of this little castle. The history of this structure remains a mystery and it is only too natural that it has fallen into its present state.

Near Montbazon, the Indre Valley narrows between two picturesque and sometimes steep hills. On a crest above the trees and roofs of the village, a keep shored up by rounded buttresses dominates the valley with its mass.

On the edge of the plateau, above the river, a handsome and solitary farm draws our attention. Its name alone is a poem: "The Beautiful Cane-Brake." It seems to be standing in the middle of the fields, showing on the side of the country rather plain, low façades flanked by stocky round towers. The attics of the living quarters are lighted by large dormer windows with sculpted pediments, a surprising thing in this rustic residence. The charm of Touraine often lies in these discoveries, but how many refined homes, symbols of a bygone way of life, are peasant houses today !

The vast horizons of the plateau of Sainte-Maure slope toward the Indre Valley at Cormery, which was the birthplace of an abbey that was famous from the twelfth to the seventeenth century. Although ruined or largely spoiled by the different uses to which they have been put, the remains of the abbatial buildings are worth visiting. They are moreover considerable enough to allow us to make a mental reconstitution of the abbey. Strolling in the little streets, you will discover a tower, the arcades of a

cloister, convent buildings and a deconsecrated abbatial church. Today the village sleeps among these vestiges, joining them to a tight network of homes in a setting of running water, broad meadows and groves.

The Indre receives, not far from there, a tumultuous and vagabond stream, the Indrois, whose valley will give us the occasion to run away and get lost!

The Indrois Valley

Perched at the meeting place of the two rivers, Follaine, a little manor-house of the fifteenth century, charms us by its name which is reminiscent of some folly. Down below the rapid Indrois rushes between ashes and service trees, swollen by the many streams that dash down from the plateau. In a splendid wooded glen little Montpoupon castle seems like a dream; a perhaps excessive restoration has changed it into a parody of a fortress.

L'Estang, isolated in a great forest, is better preserved: the fifteenth century residence is lighted by mullioned windows surmounted with high dormer windows with crockets. The side wing is adorned, as at Blois, with a gallery whose arcades are supported by twisted pillars. At the edge of this great forested area, the Indrois flows beside the ruins of the charter-house of Liget and the fortified house of Courroirie, before crossing a more open valley.

This valley is marked by villages typical of Touraine: Genillé, Saint-Quentinon-Indrois and Villeloin-Coulangé which are each richened by a church, a château or a collegiate church. Sovereign of this tiny valley, Montrésor overlooks the Indrois from the cliff on which stands the castle built in the fifteenth century by Imbert de Bastarnay on the site of a fortress. The very simple living quarters with high dormer windows retain an imposing, austere look marked by the Gothic tradition. The collegiate church, only a hundred meters (333 feet) away, contrasts with the castle by its handsome Renaissance style. Begun in the early sixteenth century, it was finished only in 1541, a fact that explains the alliance of traditional architecture and Italianized decoration. The gable has let into it a double door with depressed archways flanked by columns and surmounted by a row of niches with pillars. All these features are decorated with foliage, candelabra and arabesques whose low relief and delicate outlines call to mind the sculpted features of Azay-le-Rideau. The inside reminds us of an immense greenhouse where light flows in from the high windows, lighting up the recumbent statues on the tombs of the Bastarnays, in the back of the church. This collegiate church is one of the most remarkable examples of religious architecture of the early Renaissance in Touraine.

After Montrésor, the Indrois splits in places into several arms whose green valleys are broken up by wooded areas. Let's leave this hedge-lined path, cross the forest and so return to the banks of the Indre at Loches, a large and famous city in the valley. Laid out in tiers at the foot the castle, its silhouette is chopped up by turrets, bell-towers, sharp gables of living quarters bristling with dormer windows and ramparts. Centuries have passed over this city without leaving any deep marks or irremediable destruction, only wearing down here and there its old stones, and making them more gentle.

You enter the old town through the fortified gate of the Cordeliers (Franciscans), the vestige of the fifteenth-century perimeter wall. To the right, above more recent houses, rises St. Antony's Tower, a Renaissance bell-tower surmounted by a lantern-topped cupola; at the upper end of "main street" one sees Picoys Gate and the front of the town hall among the hodge-podge of pointed roofs. The site of the castle, which is made up of the king's quarters, St. Ursus's (Saint-Ours) collegiate church and the former keep, overlooks the valley and crowns the city. This great block is surrounded by a jumble of high perimeter walls and curtain-walls overgrown with vegetation.

From the king's quarters, one can see as far as the great forest of Loches and toward the meadows on the banks of the Indre. The façades of the castle bear the trace of two phases in the royal construction: the first in the early fifteenth century, the second in a later century. The first living quarters have a crude military look, but the second block with its dormer windows and its ermine-tufted oratory is more attractive. This wing is flanked by a slim turret called the Agnes Sorel Tower, for it contains the young woman's tomb with her recumbent statue. Behind, at the highest part of the crag, St. Ursus's collegiate church points toward the sky its two spired towers and its two curious hollow octagonal pyramids. To the south, closing the perimeter wall, a formidable eleventh-century keep defies time. The old city at the foot of the castle, with its rows of houses chopped up by narrow streets, steep alleys and stairs, forms a rather picturesque maze. The line of pointed gables is sometimes broken by a Renaissance façade like that of the Chancellery. Sixteenth-century structures are indeed rather rare at Loches. After the Hundred Years War, then the death of Charles VII, the kings forsook the town which went to sleep to dream of great times gone by.

Leaving Loches, we pass near the Renaissance château of Sausac on our way to Beaulieu-lès-Loches. Above the green pastures enclosed in the arms of the river, the spire of the twelfth-century abbatial church points to the sky. Of this Romanesque structure only the bell-tower and five arms of the transept remain, but St. Lawrence's chapel and several old houses are still intact. To the south, the classical château of Verneuil stands on the bank of the Indre, its regular façades crowned with triangular pediments and a four-sided dome. It appears suddenly as you round a bend in the road, with a long lane of linden-trees leading up to it. A few kilometers from there are found the important vestiges of the fortress of Bridoré. Here is an unexpected side of Touraine: that of military constructions, which enclose the province and which were built during the troubled times of the feudal period. It is a border region, more suited to defensive structures than to country houses. The Indre is from this point on a part of Berry, less moderate, wilder and more tumultuous than in Touraine. It flows through a deep, narrow valley between grey limestone cliffs. On one of them you see Palluau, a small medieval town whose castle has handsome Gothic façades. In a less turbulent setting, Isle-Savary at Clion is one of the region's important buildings. Leaving the road by a dirt path, you will better appreciate the vast display of the living quarters around the main courtyard. Built in the late fifteenth century, it is composed of a long rectangular pavilion with a square tower at each corner, one of them serving as keep. The entire building is crowned with a line of tall machicolations and retains its haughty defensive look.

The Indre and the Cher demarcate here a region rich in castles, of which the most famous is imposingly large Valençay. Situated on broad terraces overlooking the Nahon valley, it is a building dating from the second half of the sixteenth century. It is composed of two large blocks of living quarters, arranged in an L-shape and connected by an enormous round tower crowned by a dome. Inside, the

170

appartments enclose a handsome collection of Empire furniture. One hall is exclusively devoted to the historical souvenirs of the Prince of Talleyrand, who owned the château in the early nineteenth century.

In the park which extends westward from the château and slopes softly down to the valley, llamas, deer, cranes and flamingos run free.

Its smaller, unknown neighbor, the château of Veuil, was no doubt much more precious and refined but it has suffered a great deal from being deserted. Of this Renaissance structure, only one wing remains, which has on the ground floor a gallery of low arcades whose decoration is comparable to that of the châteaux of the Loire.

The pearl of this border region between Touraine and Berry is uncontestably Argy. Built in the late fifteenth or early sixteenth century, it is a transition castle which unites Gothic tradition to the early beginnings of the Renaissance. As is the case at Meillant, it is enriched by surprising sculpted decorations: the façades of the inner courtyard, above the gallery, are studded with initials and flat fleur-de-lys. This original decoration evokes, by its finesse and precision, the work of a goldsmith.

At the gates of "black Berry", Argy still has some of the grace and light of the Loire which has strayed into this secret country described by the "lady of Nohant".

Villegongis, an imperfect and late replica of Chambord, does not succeed in maintaining the illusion. In a melancholy setting of water and forests, it has nonetheless a particular charm when the autum wind drops on the mirror of the moat a thousand sequins of light. At Azay-le-Ferron one enters Brenne, a region of ponds and marshes, drowned in fog like Champeigne in Touraine.

The Valleys of the Creuse and the Indre

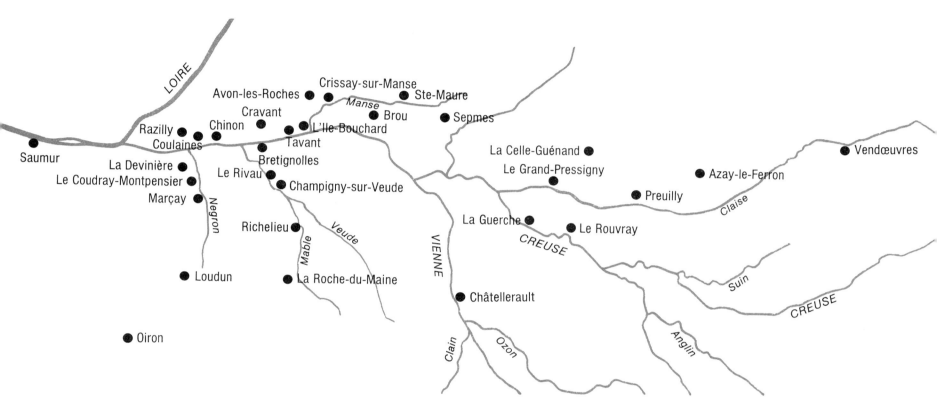

The passage between the valleys of the Creuse and the Indre is made by way of the Claise and a network of secondary streams. The Claise waters the small towns of Preuilly and Grand-Pressigny. One finds in the outskirts many important vestiges of workshops where flint was chipped and polished during the Stone Age. Preuilly, which is situated on a hill overlooking the river, is particularly rich in interesting monuments. One finds in a limited area a fifteenth-century castle, the ruins of a fortress, a collegiate church and a Romanesque abbatial church. Although the surrounding countryside is rather poor, one can still discover a few interesting

things. On the road to Chambon, one sees Rouvray, a country seat typical of Touraine, which has undergone few changes since its construction.

The most important castle in the southern part of Touraine is Grand-Pressigny. It stands on an admirable site, protected by a square keep thirty-five meters (approximately 117 feet) high. The living quarters, which were built in the sixteenth century, are lighted by high mullioned windows which are framed by columns with Ionic capitals. The vaulted gallery occupies the entire ground floor and opens onto the inner courtyard. Two tall slim turrets flank this block of living quarters, punctuating with a lighter note the stern façades. Inside, you can visit the museum of prehistory.

North of Preuilly, the Claise adds its waters to those of the Creuse, a mountain river which serves a natural boundary between Touraine and Poitou. Here a fortified castle, Guerche, built on the river banks, possesses an efficient defensive apparatus with thick towers crowned with machicolations and, underground, its casemates. This place gives a certain image of the Touraine countryside: the quiet, tranquil village is unaware of passing time, grouped as it is around a château hidden behind the trees, and the river's calm mirror reflects the moving image of the façades and pointed roofs.

The Creuse flows by the cliffs of Poitou and widens its valley in the direction of Touraine. Southward, the hill is covered with woods and thick underbrush, while to the north, the terraces of grain and meadows rise gently to the edge of the plateau. Among the many small streams rushing down to the Creuse, one has a savory name: the Aigronne. Rocky spurs, which are somewhat unexpected in this region, frame it as they jut out over the aggressive sites where medieval fortresses stand. La Celle-Guenand and Chatelier are two fairly typical examples of military architecture. In grey weather they look like Rhenish burgs.

Near the "Spit of the Two Waters", the meeting place of the Creuse and the Vienne, the modest valley of the Esves is enriched by a more attractive structure.

The château of Sepmes, which was built in the sixteenth century, has suffered from being deserted for so long, but it is now coming back to life due to an intelligently made restoration. It was built by a minor lord of Touraine who was for a time the beneficiary of both royal favor and royal gold. This protection explains the lavish character of the house. A handsome staircase still exists.

The Creuse Valley

Contrary to the Creuse, the Vienne flows through Touraine in a broad valley with softly sloping banks. The chalky ribs of the fairly distant and wood-bordered hills sometimes break through in patches, as at Chinon. But before crossing the Chinonais, the river flows beside the limestone plateau of Sainte-Maure. Its aridity and monotony are suddenly broken by the green countryside. In the midst of this setting so marked by gentleness and moderation, the small castle of Brou is well integrated. Although successive remodellings have changed the original character of this Gothic edifice, the general aspect has been preserved. The outer façade, which is, exceptionally for Touraine, the most elaborately decorated, opens onto the valley. The fortunate builders had understood that one could make use of the harmony of the countryside and the whiteness of the building materials.

The luminosity of the buildings, in this southerly part of Touraine, is due to the quality and color of the stone. In the fifteenth and sixteenth centuries it came from a nearby quarry, located near Sainte-Maure in the Courtineau Valley. The slightly ocher ecru color catches the sun and clothes the most modest structures in light. Thus appear the houses of a very small village located on the slope of a plateau whose view opens onto the Valley of the Vienne. Crissay-on-Manse, a protected site today, is a group of old well-preserved buildings which are built of the material usually used only for the houses of nobles. The traveller curious to discover Touraine may wander over the entire Valley of the Manse.

After Crissay, the hills become steeper around Roches-Tranchelions where ruins still remain of a Gothic castle and a Renaissance collegiate church. The church of the neighboring village, Avon-les-Roches, is a rather remarkable Romanesque edifice: its porch has semi-circular arcades, whose sculptured archivolts are supported by little columns with historiated capitals. This part of Touraine is rich in examples of Romanesque art: the Benedictine abbey of Bois-Aubry, the ruins of St. Leonard's at Ile-Bouchard, the church of Parçay-on-Vienne. The latter has a front door whose curves are decorated with strange bearded figures alternating with foliage, palmettes, beading and nail-head ornamentation. The richness of this decoration reveals the proximity of Poitou, as at St. Leonard's where the capitals carved in the shape monsters call to mind those of Chauvigny.

And yet, in the south of Touraine the most important example of Romanesque art is the little church of Tavant. To the beauty of the sculpted decoration is added a group of perfectly preserved frescoes. The building has kept a great deal of charm due to the little cemetery that lies next to it and the beautiful lane that leads to the western façade. We enter through an arched doorway, flanked by blind arcades and topped with three elaborately decorated arches. In the nave several interesting capitals remain, but the frescoes of the crypt are the most curious part of the church. Scenes from the Old and New Testaments are to be seen side by side with those of secular inspiration; the themes evoked, whether religious or not, are an inventory of universalist thought during the Romanesque period. You will appreciate the skill of the drawing which is accentuated by the use of a limited range of colors: ocher, green, white and black.

Overlooking the Valley of the Vienne upstream from Chinon, Brétignoles manor-house rises above a grassy slope. One sees this fine house behind a large iron gate framed by smaller gates for pedestrians. Among the many old houses in the Chinonais this is one of the best preserved. The living quarters, lighted by mullioned windows and surmounted with dormer windows, are flanked by towers without machicolations. In the center of the façade, a polygonal staircase turret gives this manor-house the last touch necessary to make it look like a country home. Before Chinon, the alluvial terraces on either side of the Vienne are covered with vineyards and orchards. Ligré, Cravant and

174

Panzoult, all charming little villages, are also the names of great vintages of this wine country.

Then Chinon appears in the sun, stretching out on a chalky cliff the silhouette of its ruined castle. At its feet, the "little town of renown" extends from the cliff to the Vienne, forming a landscape of mainly horizontal lines. The vestiges of the three castles occupy a rocky spur overlooking the river, cut off on the south by a sheer cliff and limited on the north by a deep, narrow dale. The structures take the shape of this natural site and are arranged in a long complicated rectangle of fortifications and defensive works. Of the castle, which was demolished in the early nineteenth century, there remain only the vestiges we see today: the Clock Tower, Coudray Tower and Fort St. George; you must make a great effort to imagine what the buildings were like. Coming from the town, after having climbed a ramp you enter the fortress by the eastern gate of Fort St. George then cross the drawbridge before walking under the Clock Tower. The latter opened onto the "middle castle", in which the king's quarters were located. At the extreme west end there was a fortified redoubt, called Fort du Coudray, in one of whose towers Joan of Arc stayed. And yet, because your reconstitution of the castle is imperfect, you may dream in the shade of a section of wall where a chimney hangs in empty space, and imagine poor Charles VIII, hunted and spied upon, suspiciously receiving this young unknown girl who had come to help him get his

kingdom back. During the Hundred Years War, Chinon lived its last great hours. Peace was to leave it useless and out of style. Time and the forgetfulness of human beings were to complete the ruin of this now deserted royal domain.

As you come down from the castle the old town invites you for a stroll along Voltaire Street, at the foot of the cliff. A series of old stone or half-timbered houses constitutes a group of exceptional unity. Many houses are surrounded by minuscule courtyards and small gardens hanging from the rock which are overrun by Virginia creeper, ivy and wisteria. A few handsome churches are to be seen as you stroll through the old quarter: the former church of St. Mexme, now only half its earlier size, is Romanesque; St. Maurice's owes its fame to its vault of very pure Angevin style and St. Stephen's to its fine flamboyant door.

It is impossible to speak of Chinon without mentioning its nearby forest, whose immensity also hides a few handsome ruins. The abbeys of Turpenay and Pommier Aigre (Sour Apple Tree) are today in ruins, but as you go looking for them you will have a long walk on the path of Louis XI's hunting lodge, Forges de Bonaventure.

Once back at Chinon, before crossing the Vienne and reaching the other bank, you must make a detour to Véron. Situated between the Loire and the Vienne, this flat country of the watershed of both rivers possesses castles that are in the main unknown. Velors, being too close to a tentacular power plant and hidden by a curtain of trees, can hardly be seen from the road. The castle was built in the late fifteenth century and enlarged in the seventeenth century with pavilions and outbuildings. One reaches the main courtyard through a monumental gate. Closing the courtyard, the fifteenth-century living quarters show a white façade dotted with bricks in no particular geometrical pattern as at Chatigny or Réaux. This local decorative device is used here with great imagination! All the charm of Velors is due to this original decoration and to the luminosity of its façades in the sun. You have only to cross the highroad to find another manor-house, Baronnière, which has been forgotten by everyone.

On the Véron soil the density of late medieval and Renaissance castles and manor-houses is amazing: Destilly, Razilly, Coulaine and Courtinière, whose musical names alone call to mind houses that were agreeable to live in. In spite of its being deserted and defaced, Courtinière has kept a little of its splendor of former days. Built in mid-sixteenth century, it boasts a military apparatus of crenelles and machicolations, made unseemly by the profuse sculptured decorations. This richness is surprising on such a small structure. It is one of the last castles before the junction of the Vienne and the Loire at Candes. Véron, a little tongue of land bounded by the two rivers, ends here. To appreciate the countryside you must climb the steep slopes of the cliff behind the Candes church. From there you can see during the summer low tides sandbanks between which the two rivers try to meet. The fall and spring floods, which inundate this flat country, keep you from seeing this watershed, but give another aspect of it. On the other bank of the Vienne is Rabelais's country, a moderate and amiable soil, suited to delicate crops. The little valley of the Ligron at Devinière, where Rabelais was born, was the setting of the Picrocholean War, but other places call to mind these imaginary battles: Lerné, Seuilly and La Roche-Clermaut, which were the important places in the world of Rabelais's characters.

Le Coudray-Montpensier castle seems to be a part of this world. From a high hill, its aggressive towers overlook Seuilly and the entire Chinon countryside. You enter this fifteenth century moat-encircled fortress through a gate let into a tall square tower. The stern block of living quarters is flanked by tall buttressed towers which are crowned with merlons. Few castles in Touraine, except for Langeais, still have so defensive an appearance.

Opposite Chinon, the hill on the left bank, which is fairly distant from the river, is covered with forests. On this background of greenery stand out the light-colored façades of La Vauguyon, Plessis-Gerbault and Vaugaudry. The abundance of these little castles, the beauty of the most humble farms as well as the richness of the soil and the mildness of the climate make of the area around Chinon a real land of milk and honey. At some distance from the Vienne, Marçay typifies this architecture of the Chinonais. This fifteenth-century edifice, which was rebuilt and remodelled in the sixteenth century, unites the vestiges of feudal elegance to the novelties of the country house: the combination of two absolutely different ways of life which gives these houses an original character.

On the banks of the Veude, a small tributary of the Vienne, Le Rivau is one of the castles of the Chinonais that have suffered least from restorations. In spite of the disappearance of the chapel and the razing of some of the living quarters, it still has a great deal of character. The thirteenth-century keep, proudly standing in the southern part, contains the carriage entrance of the drawbridge. The large block of living quarters, facing eastward, is flanked by two cylindrical towers at the corners and a polygonal turret in the center of the façade. To the north, a little square pavilion has a gate topped with a watch turret. In the outbuildings are semi-circular barrel-vaulted stables and in the courtyard a Renaissance fountain with a broad basin.

To the south, toward the lands of the Richelais and their vast horizons, Champigny-on-Veude retains only the memory of its castle. Richelieu, a jealous neighbor, ordered its destruction in the early seventeenth century. In the park, the Sainte-Chapelle fortunately escaped this delirium of destruction. Begun in 1510 and finished in 1548, it is of Gothic conception but its decoration is inspired by Renaissance themes. The entrance is preceded by a peristyle with pilasters and columns supporting the entablature which is ornamented with a frieze. The walls are richly decorated with garlands, medallions and niches containing statues. But the main interest of this seigniorial chapel lies in the magnificent Renaissance stained glass which fills the tall windows with flamboyant color. Not far from there, on a hill, a country lord had built during the reign of Louis XIV an immense château, La Grillière, whose long stone façade is stretched out on a single level and topped by attics where dormer windows alternate with small circular windows. The forepart of the building, topped with a triangular pediment, accentuates the center of the structure and gives it classical majesty which is unexpected in this unpretentious countryside.

The region has been subject to excessive projects. It was a few kilometers from there that Cardinal de Richelieu conceived the project of a new town and a palace. The little town that dozes today in the heart of the Richelais is spread over a rectangle 700 meters long and 500 meters wide (approximately 2333 feet by 1666 feet). It is arranged around the main avenue which serves as the central axis for identical mansions and cross-streets. The château, the work of the architect Lemercier, was demolished during the Restoration. Only a few parts have been spared: the entrance pavilion, the orange greenhouse and the outbuildings which can still be seen in the handsome park.

After Richelieu, we leave Touraine for the Loudunais or region of Loudun, at the border of Poitou. Between Loudun and

Mirebeau, three castles still belong to the Vale of the Loire. Roche-du-Maine occupies a traditional site on a bare ridge in the middle of a plain. Surrounded by a now-dry moat, the castle, which was built around 1520, unites feudal defense elements with Renaissance decoration. The latter, of a richness common in the Vale of the Loire, is carried out in fine stone of exceptional quality. Its neighbor, the château of Coussay, situated on the rolling hills of the Mirebelais, was built in the early sixteenth century by an important burger of Touraine who had become a prelate. The decoration, like that at Azay-le-Rideau, is limited to the dormer windows and to the window and door facings and can stand comparison with that of the château on the banks of the Indre. The flexibility of the design and the finesse of relief of the foliage and arabesques give this edifice incomparable grace. At the entrance to the forecourt on the side of the farm buildings, an elegant pavilion contains a fountain where the refinement of the sculpted decoration is inexplicable considering the use to which the building was put. South of Loudun, Oiron, situated in the heart of a vast plain, can be seen from very far away. The château displays the juxtaposition of a Renaissance wing and a large classical pavilion built in the seventeenth century on the site of a former dwelling house. The Renaissance structure, which was begun in 1516, was finished only in 1559. The remaining part opens on the ground floor onto a gallery whose arches are supported by twisted pillars. The latter are topped with niches which formerly contained statues and terra cotta ornaments. The upper floor of this gallery, lighted by broad windows, contains a long room entirely covered with frescoes whose theme is the Trojan War. On the borders of Touraine, this pictorial group, which was directly inspired by the Gallery of Ulysses at Fontainebleau, surprises us by its size and allows us to imagine the luxurious life in the province during the sixteenth century.

The Loir Valley

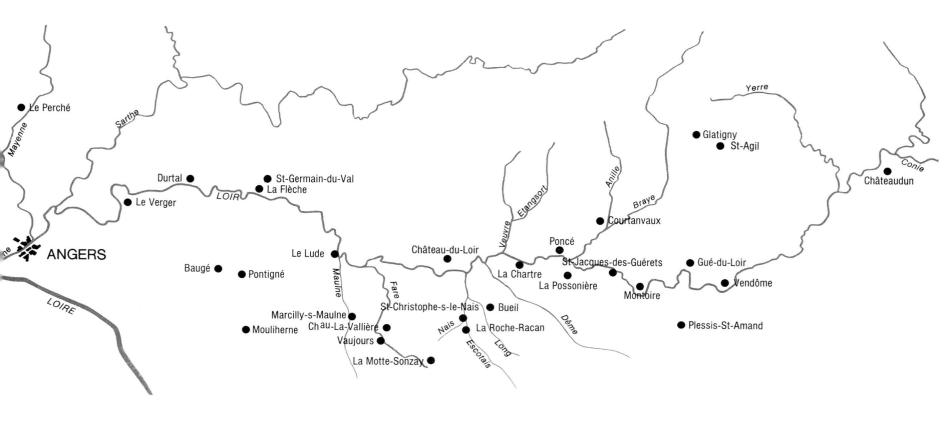

The north of the Vale of the Loire is bounded by a single waterway, the Loir, which serves as natural boundary to Anjou, Touraine and the Blesois. It is a different river from the tributaries of the south, whose valleys break the monotony of the plateau. It flows slowly in a wide valley. Its loops and meanders are edged with rows of trees, pollard oaks, willows and young elms, which signal its presence from afar.

The landscape, with is sometimes monotonous in Anjou and in northern Touraine, is not without charm here. In winter, the high waters overflow onto the vast prairie. Over the sleeping countryside then spreads the heavy silence of the flooded plains broken only at times by a

bird's cry. Near Vendôme, the relief is more rugged, and the Loir flows around hills, cliffs and promontories. Sometimes rounding a loop or a steep crag, you come upon a mill, a keep or a castle showing its blue-roofed outline.

Near its junction with the Sarthe, the valley, deeper now, was the site of one of the region's most beautiful castles. Le Verger, now in ruins, is known through many seventeenth century drawings which enable us to imagine the magnificence of the residence. Built in the late fifteenth century by Pierre de Rohan, it bore some ressemblance to an Angevin castle already mentioned, Plessis-Bourré. The latter exercised a definite influence on Le Verger, particularly in the disposition of the living quarters between two low wings.

Following the valley in the direction of Durtal, we find the Loir full of charm. On its banks ends the forest of Chambiers, one of the most beautiful and largest in Anjou. Durtal, built in the sixteenth century by a companion of Francis I, is a formidable edifice which rises from a promontory above the river. Between Durtal and Baugé, the more pleasant Gastines is now freed of the modern structures that crushed it and appears graceful and charming. Built under Henry II, it is a rustic manor-house whose beauty resides mainly in the fine proportions of its buildings of unequal heights. Baugé, although it is far from the Loir, occupies a particular position in the heart of the Angevin forests. In the center of an agreeable town stands the castle built by Yolanda of Aragon on the site of an older fortress. Remodelled later by her son René of Anjou, it is in no way a sumptuous edifice. It is an unostentatious gentleman's home, whose elegant flamboyant decoration is at its most splendid in the great staircase. The town retains a few vestiges of this royal past: a curious church surmounted by a spiral steeple and a hospital with its seventeenth century pharmacy.

On the outskirts, we discover handsome churches, like the one at Pouligné, which is decorated with frescoes, and the one at Bocé where Romanesque sculpture ennobles the façade. At Mouliherne, the twelfth-century church is covered with one of the first Angevin vaults. Near La Flèche, the well-named village, Saint-Germain-du-Val-Perché (St. Germain of the Hanging Valley), is worth a visit because of its location overlooking the Loir Valley as far as Lude.

Lude, a fortress built by the Daillon family, commanded the access to the Loir during the Hundred Years War. Its reconstruction was undertaken in the late fifteenth century but was finished only at the end of the following century. The castle is composed of four wings with a tower at each corner, forming a square inner courtyard. The history of the construction is too complex to be summarized and you will be more sensitive here to the setting of greenery than to architectural matters. The gardens and terraces that slope down to the Loir surround the castle in a jewel box of water and vegetation. The loops of the river encircle the building, illuminating it with dancing light.

Before reaching Château-du-Loir, the Loir swallows up an infinity of streams which take their source in northern Touraine. The Maulne, the Escotais, the Nais and the Dême have small valleys which often hold the surprise of a château, a picturesque village or a church. On the Maulne, Marcilly is totally forgotten, situated as it is at the northernmost point of Touraine; it was built during the first years of the seventeenth century. The majestic appearance of the structure and its regular plan announce the coming of the classical period. To the south, near Château-la-Vallière, a forest hides the ruins of a

vallée du cher

valley of the cher
Tal des Cher

CHARLES VII ROY ... DE FRANCE

103/104 . Meillant

◄ 102 . Montrichard.

Bourges . 105/106 ►

114/116 . Sologne.
115 . Cheverny.

117 . Sologne.
118 . La Ferté-Beauharnais.

119 . Monthou-sur-Cher.
120 . Fougères-sur-Bièvre.
121 . Saint-Aignan.

Fougères-sur-Bièvre . 122 ▶

123/124 . Lassay-sur-Croisne.
Château du Moulin.
125 . Le Gué-Péan.

126 / 127 . Chenonceau.

128 / 129 / 130 . Chenonceau.

Chenonceau . 131 ▶

132 . Villandry.

133 . Villandry.

vallée de l'indre

valley of the indre
Tal der Indre

135 / 136 . Azay-le-Rideau.

◄ 134 . Courçay.

137 . Azay-le-Rideau.

138 . Montbazon.
139 . Le Grand-Pressigny.
140 . Ussé.

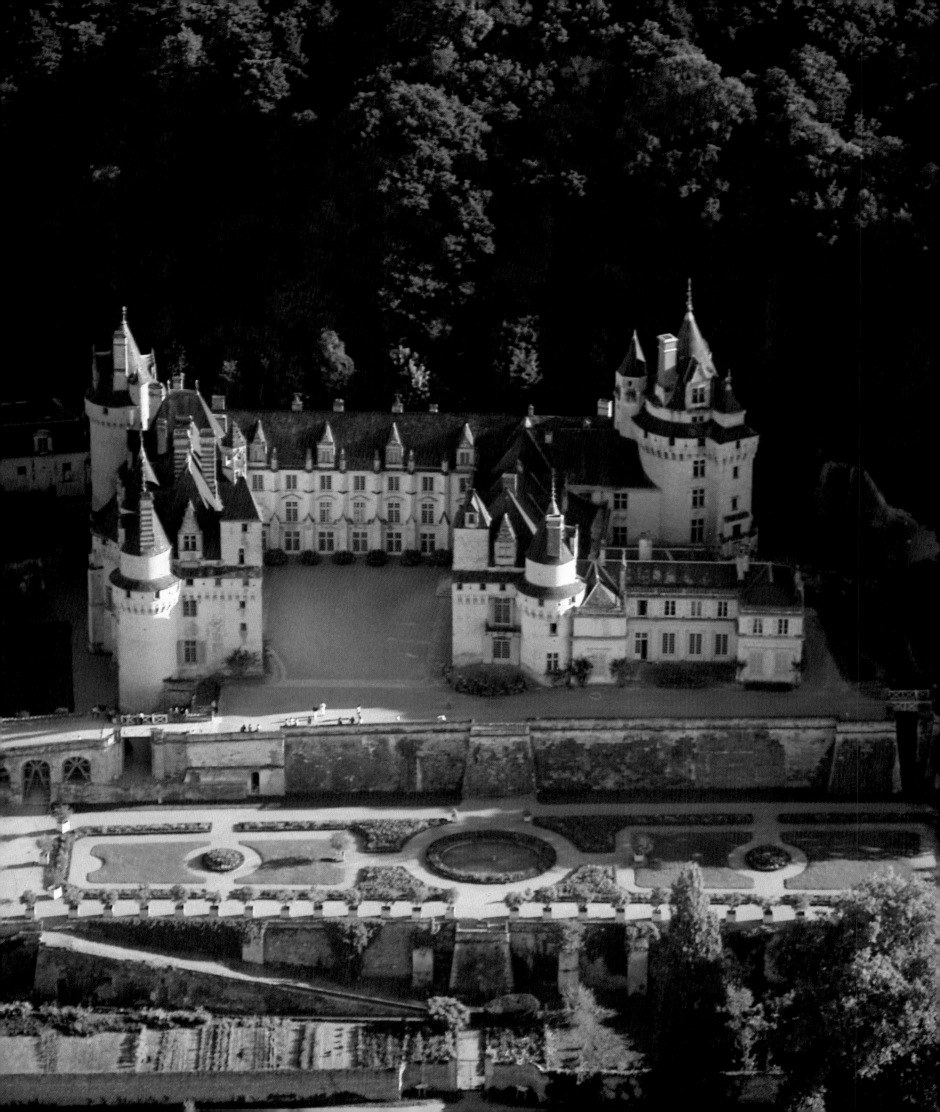

141 . Valençay.
142 . Saché.
143 . Montpoupon.

144 . L'Indrois.
145 . La Courroirie.
146 . Montrésor.

147 . Loches.

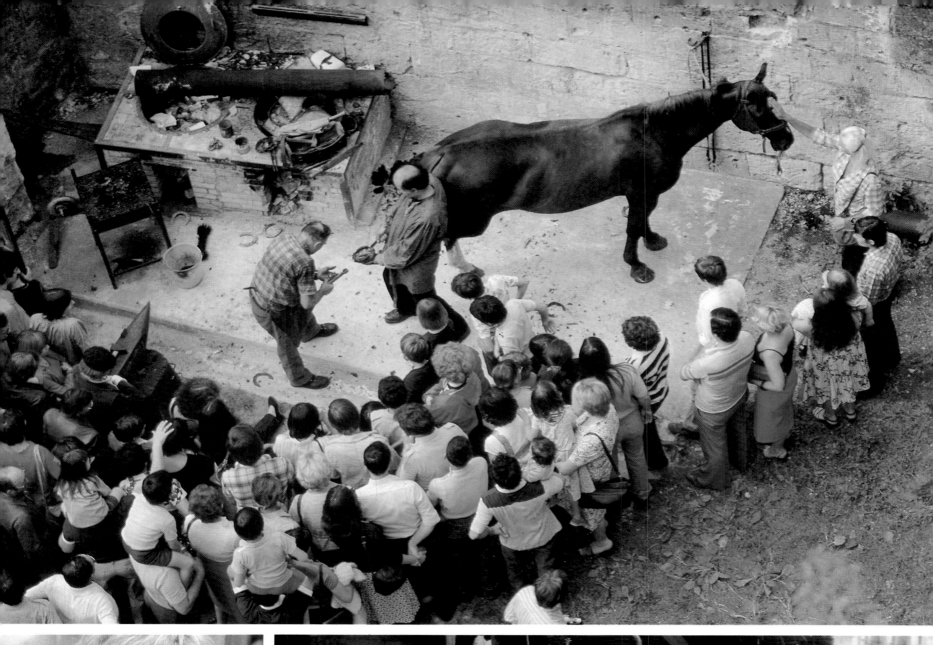

vallées de la creuse et de la vienne

valleys of the creuse and the vienne
Tal der Creuse und Tal der Vienne

RUE
BRETONNEAU

156 . Chinon.
157 . Richelieu.

158 . Le Rivau.
159/160 ► Champigny-sur-Veude.

vallée du loir

valley of the loir
Tal des Loir

165 . Le Lude.

fortress. Vaujours, once called Val Joyeux, stands in the hollow of a deep, narrow wooded valley. The beauty of the site is in keeping with the fanciful sight of cracked tower walls and razed perimeter walls surrounded by marshes.

At the source of the Fare, La Motte-Sonzay, a solid structure with corner towers, would call to mind some sudden attack of the Hundred Years War if its façade had not been remodelled in the Renaissance style. In the surrounding countryside, a country seat which charms us by the sound of its name, Naudésir, rises above the Valley of the Escotais. The main living quarters have remained unchanged since their construction in the late sixteenth century. Surrounded by a broad moat, it is topped by a steep roof with beautiful dormer windows with double openings. The regular façade with pilaster-framed, mullioned windows let into it makes us think of moderation and harmony.

The neighboring château of Roche-Racan belonged, as its name indicates, to the poet Racan who had it rebuilt in the seventeenth century. It is integrated into a splendid landscape of water and greenery, an association native to Touraine, as we know.

The course of the Long, a vagabond stream, leads us to our last stop in northern Touraine, the village of Bueil. It has two very interesting churches: the parish church of St Peter of the Bonds and the collegiate church, St. Michael's. The former, begun in 1480 and consecrated in 1512, is richly decorated in a style typical of the early Renaissance. In the nave, sixteenth-century baptismal fonts are composed of stone basins topped with elaborately carved wooden lids. The latter church was founded in the late fourteenth century and has a sixteenth-century crypt which before the French Revolution contained recumbent statues on the tombs of the Bueil family.

After this short incursion into Touraine, we rejoin the Loir at La Chartre where it divides into several arms and encloses the town. Not far from there is Poncé, which owes its fame to a magnificent Renaissance staircase whose straight flights are covered with coffered vaulting. The latter are decorated with lively, fanciful motifs: coats-of-arms, cupids and salamanders alternate with masks, medallions, mascarons and a profusion of plant elements. Numbering 136 and all different, they constitute this manor-house's only luxury. Opposite the château the terraces overlooking the Loir are planted with a curious labyrinth of yoke-elms arranged around a hundred-year-old plane tree. The Romanesque village church is decorated with frescoes like most Loir Valley churches. After Poncé the landscape broadens and the wider horizon permits us to see the first curves of the Vendômois. Between Poncé and Vendôme, other châteaux, fortresses and churches make each village an interesting place.

La Possonière manor-house was the cradle of the Ronsard family. The rather modest living quarters, dating from the early sixteenth century, are enriched by a door a dormer window of great refinement. Inside is a highly decorated Renaissance chimney, one of the best preserved of the Loire Valley. The courtyard is bounded on the east by a rocky mass housing seven caves whose entrances were decorated in the sixteenth century with mottoes and sayings engraved on lintels. The poet's parents were cultivated people, art lovers and humanists. The house descended to Ronsard's brother but the poet stayed there frequently; he sang in many poems of this Loir Valley.

From La Possonière to Vendôme it is called the "valley of frescoes" because of the many Romanesque churches decorated with murals. Saint-Jacques-des-Guérets is the best-known one because of the variety of painted scenes there and the beauty of the colors. The coppery tones are reminiscent of miniatures and are closer to Gothic painting than to the Romanesque shades seen in the region. Troo, a curious troglodyte village, has a Romanesque chapel decorated with frescoes. It is overshadowed by its neighbor, Saint-Gilles-de-Montoire. Situated in the suburb of Saint-Oustrille this private chapel is now half in ruins. The frescoes covering its walls are considered the most beautiful Romanesque paintings of the valley. The free-flowing movement and the lightness of the colors make them an exceptional ensemble.

Montoire is built on a hill at the summit of which stands a ruined keep and it is encircled by a loop of the Loir. Near the town at the place called Bois-Freslon, a fortified manor-house stands on a wooded hill. Further away, Courtanvaux castle has

an agreeable name that is not belied by the structure itself. It surprises us by the dazzling whiteness of its façades which we discover beyond a monumental entrance flanked by towers. The region is well provided with fortresses and keeps! Taking the direction of Lavardin, we see from afar the impressive square tower called the "Shoulder". Gigantic and perched on a great rock, these ruins look like fragments of enormous bones. The parish church presents a complete panorama of mural painting of the twelfth of the fifteenth century.

Near Vendôme the Loir's loops increase in number. At Gué-du-Loir it waters Bonaventure manor-house, now only a modest farm which, like the song, is forgotten. Vendôme was the cradle of the powerful counts of the same name, one of France's greatest feudal families until the sixteenth century. We enter the town by St. George's gate, which is flanked by two big towers dating from the fourteenth century, and whose opening was widened in the last century to permit the passage of a national highway. Handsome churches in a large park, the castle ruins and a few dwelling houses maintain the ancient character of this town. The present Ronsard Lycée, a college for Oratorian fathers founded in the seventeenth century by César de Vendôme, is situated in a garden washed by the Loir. In town, bridges and foot-bridges span the river which is ramified into several branches.

The town's jewel is Trinity church, which was built from the fourteenth to the sixteenth century. It is surmounted by a very tall bell-tower whose proportions symbolize formal perfection. The choir and the front façade are masterpieces of flamboyant Gothic art. Inside, magnificient stained glass enlivens the tall windows and the splendid rose window in the entrance. The stone screen that separates the choir from the ambulatory and the fountain from the nave is from the Renaissance period.

Outside of Vendôme the Loir encircles hills and promontories, speckled with villages dug into the rock. Although the valley looks very much the same, the surrounding countryside changes little by little. Vast stretches of treeless land foretell the wheatfields of Beauce. The light is more mineral-like and the wind, unhampered by any grove of trees, sometimes swells the waves of grain.

In this land of clay where stone is rare, the buildings are of a different color: pink brick has replaced white tufa. Near Vendôme, Vievy-le-Rayé, Renay, Glatigny and Saint-Agil, with its refined Renaissance decoration, are made of brick. Modest as it is in appearance, this material gives the buildings a melancholy touch as at Plessis-Saint-Amand. This Louis XIII château, with its brick walls and stone ties, is a place that calls to mine a poetic reminiscence, a "fancy" of Gérard de Nerval:

"Then a brick château with stone corners
With windowglass stained in reddish colors,
Girded by great parks with a river..."

The end of the poem is very sad and we can't leave the laughing Loir Valley on such a disenchanted note.

Chateaudun, in spite of its northerly situation, should, because of its castle, be associated with the art of the Loire. The town occupies a strategic situation on a steep rock. Built by Dunois in the fifteenth century, the imposing fortress overlooks the valley.

The thick walls which grip the rock solidly and are shored up by buttresses, have nothing of the Loire's gentleness. We will understand the relationship only after having entered the courtyard: a delightful flamboyant chapel leans against the ancient keep while ancient L-shaped living quarters close the perimeter wall. Built in the fifteenth century, these living quarters are flanked by elegant watchtowers and a polygonal turret and have broad windows with prismatic mullioned windows. These features give a certain finesse to the building, but they are overshadowed by the wonder of the castle: a monumental staircase which joins the two wings of the living quarters and opens on each floor onto a double loggia with very fine flamboyant decoration.

All during this outing, I have wanted to tell of a unique artistic heritage. My modest purpose was to avoid limiting the Vale of the Loire to this "Renaissance land", famous because of several great châteaux that one visits traditionally. This goal will have been reached if I awake the reader's curiosity as I guide him outside the beaten paths.

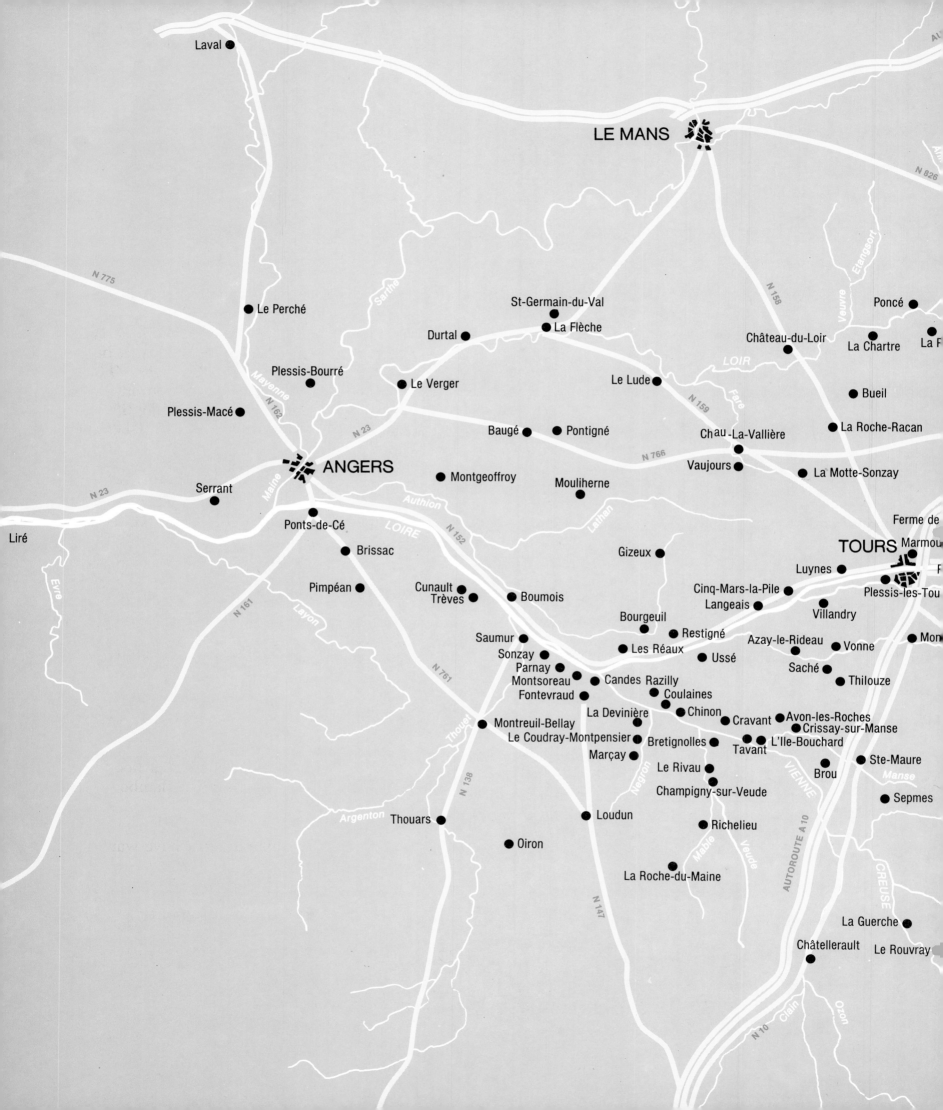

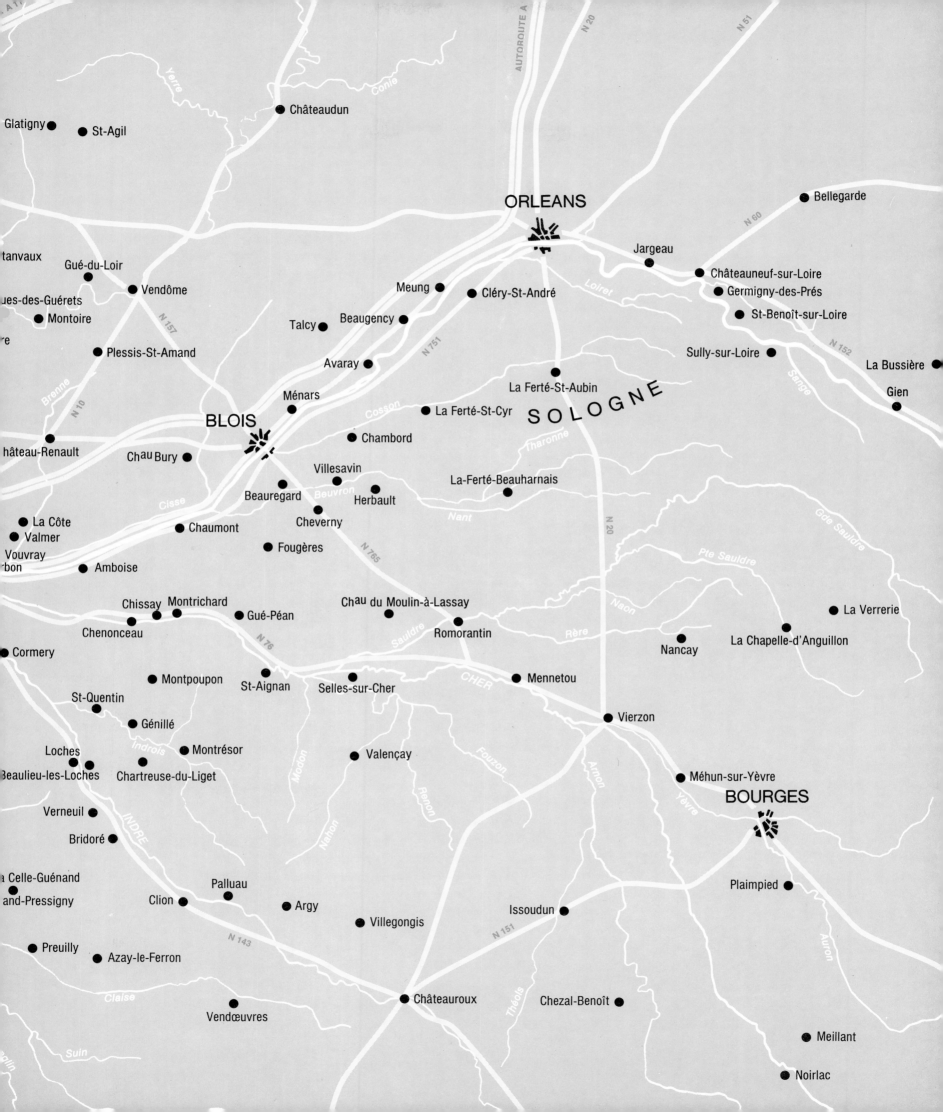

The great chateaux
of the Loire

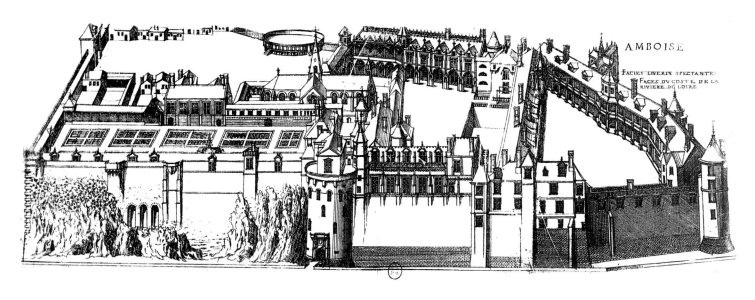

AMBOISE

Two large towers, elegant royal living quarters, the very charming St. Hubert's chapel, oratory of queens, and a terrace overlooking the Loire – this is Amboise castle, one of the greatest. Its rebirth dates from the time of Charles VIII, and Philippe de Commines tells us that the artists in charge of the gardens and buildings came from Naples. Among them was Il Boccador. The young king wanted this to be his "earthly paradise". He met his death here in 1498 after hitting his head against the lintel of a door.

Francis I used the castle for lavish parties, which may have been attended by Leonardo da Vinci, the king's friend, who lived at Clos Lucé.

A curtain falls on joy, death returns with the Amboise Conspiracy in 1560. La Renaudie's Protestants are hanged from the balconies and thrown into the Loire.

Under Louis XIV, Amboise was a prison "frequented" by Fouquet and Lauzun. During the Empire it was hardly better, Roger Ducos, a former member of the Directory, being the owner. Amboise then returned to the House of France, a branch of the Orleans family, which recently donated it to the St. Louis Foundation, whose patron the Count of Paris is.

Between 1848 and 1853 Emir Abd El-Kader, who was exiled at Amboise, was an occupant of the castle. He lived in the king's quarters, including the Hall of the Estates.

At Clos Lucé (fifteenth century), a few steps away, we can call to mind the great da Vinci; the well-preserved house is a museum devoted to his memory.

AZAY-LE-RIDEAU

It is the most characteristic of the châteaux of the Loire even though it is the Indre that feeds its moat. It was built from 1518 to 1529 for Gilles Berthelot, the king's treasurer.

After the financier Semblançay was hanged at Montfaucon, Berthelot, who was compromised in the affair, became frightened, fled and abandoned Azay to Francis I. We are still profiting from the "gift". Azay is a very pleasant and very human size. It unites the graces of the Renaissance and the rigidity of the Middle Ages: lace on a healthy skin. And the moat is placed exactly at the place where, in autumn, the leaves fall, for, of course, Azay is set among trees and its "curtain" is green or reddish-brown, according to the season.

Mullioned windows, pilasters, dormer windows and sculpted pinnacles, little columns, niches and friezes, gables and machicolations (which could almost be from an operetta) are adorned with ermines and salamanders.

The façades are splendid and the towers well placed. Harmony reigns over Azay where nothing is very surprising except the perfect success of the undertaking.

In 1870 while Francis Charles of Prussia was staying there, a chandelier fell on a table. It was feared that this was an assassination attempt and Azay barely escaped being destroyed.

One must visit it and climb the great staircase situated behind the large gable.

There is a museum of the Renaissance here; it is quite at home.

BLOIS

Sitting at the top of the city, the château is a rich lesson in architecture and history combined.

A lesson in *architecture* because after Charles d'Orléans, ex-prisoner of the English, a prince-poet who held court at Blois from 1440 to 1464 (he entertained François Villon, among others), Louis XII, his son, had the eastern façade built and placed an equestrian statue of himself there. In architecture again because Francis I, on the basis of Denis Sourdeau's plans, built the façade of the Loggias and the famous staircase, a Renaissance jewel. In architecture again because we owe to Gaston d'Orléans the seventeenth century living quarters that were designed by Mansart.

A lesson in *history* because Blois was the theater of great events: the betrothal of the future Henry IV (1572), the assassination of the Duke of Guise (1588) in Henry III's apartment (Francis I wing) and the Estates General (1576 and 1588).

Deserted for a century, in 1788 the castle became a caserne. Its restoration was begun in 1845.

Inside and outside, a long visit is a must.

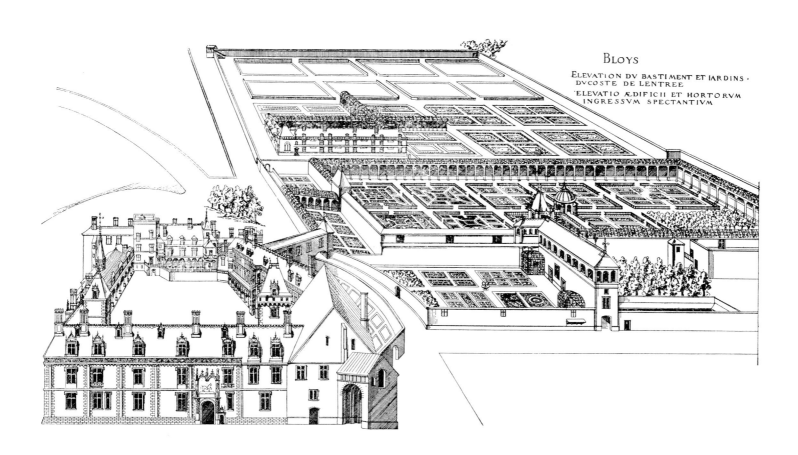

BLOYS

ELEVATION DV BASTIMENT ET IARDINS ·
DVCOSTE DE LENTREE

ELEVATIO ÆDIFICII ET HORTORVM
INGRESSVM SPECTANTIVM

CHAMBORD

Immense and yet light, singular, legendary Chambord on the Cosson is in the middle of a 5000 hectare (12,500 acre) park enclosed by thirty-two kilometers (twenty-two miles) of walls.

Francis I had the château built so that he could hunt there. For twelve years, 1800 workers labored on it.

In 1539 when Emperor Charles V came to visit, it was not completed, but the double spiral staircase had already been built. It is well-known that it permits persons going up and down to see each other through openings without meeting.

Bell-turrets, dormer windows, lantern-turrets and chimneys on the roofs oppose their extraordinary stone forest to the real forest nearby in the park.

Under Henry II the chapel was built. We shall skip other kings, even Henry IV, to find Chambord under Louis XIII in the hands of Gaston d'Orléans. But it was in 1660 under Louis XIV that Mansart did considerable remodelling to lodge the king's retinue, which allowed Molière to play *Monsieur de Pourceaugnac* and *Le Bourgeois Gentilhomme* for the first time before the court. Stanislas Leszczynski, Louis XV's father-in-law, lived here long enough to have the moat filled, which was a mistake.

Then came Field Marshal de Saxe, the victor at Fontenoy, who lodged two cavalry regiments composed of Wallachians, Tartars, Martinicans and a terrified actress named Favart.

During the Empire, Field Marshal Berthier made Chambord the "Principality of Wagram", a very curious thing to do, to say the least. Later a national subscription saved Chambord and it was given to the Duke of Bordeaux in spite of Paul Louis Courier's protests. Today Chambord belongs to the State, which bought it for 11,000,000 francs in 1932 from the heirs of the Count of Chambord.

CHAUMONT

Five towers, one of which is square. There would have been seven if one of the occupants had not wanted to have an opening onto the Loire and had the terrace built. Chaumont belonged to the Amboise family before Catherine de' Medici. It was here that the celebrated queen worked with the astrologer Ruggieri to know what the future held in store for her. Prudent and perhaps superstitious, Catherine was also vindictive. Diane of Poitiers having stolen her husband, soon after the death of Henri II Catherine forced her rival to give her Chenonceau and in turn gave Chaumont to Diane.

It was not before the eighteenth century that Chaumont was turned into a pottery under the direction of the Italian, Nini, a famous ceramist and engraver on glass, and thus came back to life.

Lovers of the medieval style will get their fill at Chaumont of towers and a drawbridge. Those who prefer the Renaissance will find a handsome well and, inside, a chapel, paneling and period floor tiles. Others can dream above the Loire which Chaumont dominates with its solid mass.

CHENONCEAU

A château-bridge on the calm Cher, but what a bridge, what a château and what gardens around them! In February, 1513, financier-baron Bohier bought the property from the Marques family and together with his wife, Catherine Briçonnet, had the château built.

Diane of Poitiers, Henry II's mistress, had the bridge built, and her rival, Catherine de' Medici, the gallery over it. When to these three lady-builders you have added the melancholy Louise of Lorraine, Henry III's widow, the inconsolable "queen in white", you will have reached the summit of womanhood in action and in prayer. Just before the Revolution came Madame Dupin whose son was tutored by Jean-Jacques Rousseau, who spoke in glowing terms of this happy time in his *Confessions*. In 1864, a Madame Pelouze bought the château and made its renovation her life's work.

If one had to give a prize for pomp to one of these ladies, it would go to Catherine de' Medici who gave magnificent parties in the days before Henry III's rustic banquet, which cost 100,000 pounds. Not long before, the Bohiers had bought the property of Chenonceau for 12,000 pounds.

In what concerns creators, we must mention the architect Philibert Delorme, who built the gallery, and Du Cerceau, who designed an extension. The present interior is decorated in beautiful Renaissance style and contains paintings and tapestries, some of which are by famous artists.

CHEVERNY

In this land of invention that the Loire country is, Cheverny's classicism is surprising but agreeably so. The unfinished southern façade has niches for busts. The completed northern façade would be austere if it were not for the handsome stone bridge spanning the moat. This residence was completed in 1634 by Henry Hurault, Count of Cheverny and son of a chancellor of Henry II and Henry IV. The de Vibraye family, another branch of the Chevernys, are the present owners.
The park is beautiful with its woods and ornamental lakes, but one must see the inside of the castle, which is remarkably rich.
Decoration, beams, elaborate chimneys, famous paintings, tapestries, drawing rooms and guardrooms, gallery and king's chamber, everything here is an art lesson.
And you may be fortunate enough to see a stag hunt when you visit Cheverny.

CHINON

Three ruined fortresses crown the rocky spur of Chinon above the Vienne. Philip Augustus, king of France, took them away from Henry II and Richard the Lion-hearted.
Charles VII, "King of Bourges", was living in the central castle when he received in the great hall a young peasant girl of eighteen, Joan of Arc, who had to discover him, somewhat disguised, among three hundred persons. Born of an inconstant mother, the dauphin doubted that he was the king's son. Joan reassured him and the war to free France began (1429).
Chinon kept the court until the middle of the fifteenth century and it was here that the Papal Legate, Caesar Borgia, came to deliver Louis XII from his first wife who was outrageously humpbacked but daughter of Louis XI. That allowed the gallant king to marry later Charles VII's widow, that Anne who brought Britanny to France.

Walking down a footpath, we can dream in these castles. The last illustrious owner was Cardinal de Richelieu.
But you must also go down into Old Chinon, which is all the more worth the trouble since one can brighten up the outing with a good red wine and the no less savory memory of Rabelais who spent his childhood at La Devinière, several miles away.

LANGEAIS

The present castle, built in a few years on the order of Louis XI, permits us to forget the razed keep of Foulques Nerra, a colorful Count of Anjou who alternated murders and repentance. Louis XI wanted Langeais to be a fortress on the route to Britanny. Fate sweetly decided otherwise, since it was at Langeais that young Anne of Britanny let herself be married to Charles VIII in 1491.
Langeais became useless as a fortress. So, over the centuries, its owners decorated it and the fortress with the fierce drawbridge was succeeded by high dormer windows, mullioned windows and octagonal towers. The terrace is the site of beautiful gardens in the French style and the apartments are noble and well furnished.

LOCHES

We are in the Middle Ages and the ghost of Agnes Sorel, who was the favorite of Charles VII, hardly blurs the armor of Richard the Lion-hearted and Philip Augustus, who fought over this fortress. The keep is a handsome structure but the Martelet will make you shudder because of its dungeons (Loches was used as a prison), in particular that of Ludovico il Moro, Duke of Milan, who was imprisoned there for eight years and died of light the day he was freed, that of the rebellious Bishops of Le Puy and Autun and that of the Count of Saint-Vallier, Diane of Poitier's father, who learned of his pardon on the gallows. In the round tower, La Ballue who had been made cardinal by Louis XI but had betrayed him to Charles the Bold, was confined in a very tight cage known as a "little girl".

St. Ursus's church with its four bell-towers of Romanesque style enables us to escape from this depravity.

Loches is a town as much as a castle. You should walk inside the medieval walls from the gates to the king's quarters while dreaming of an imaginary meeting with Thierry la Fronde or Robin Hood.

MENARS

With its gardens and terraces above the Loire, the central part of the château of Ménars dates from 1637. It was completed in 1760 according to the plans of Gabriel and then of Soufflot. The flower-beds are said to be by Le Nôtre.

The Taillemans, the Testus, the Hercule de Bidours and especially the Charrons were the successive owners of the château before the most illustrious, Madame de Pompadour, who kept the property for four years. Her brother, the Marquis de Marigny, succeeded her. He held open house there for scholars until his death in 1781.

In spite of the delapidation it suffered during the Revolution, Ménars still has a proud air and its sloping gardens owe as much to their natural situation overlooking the Loire as to the work done by human beings.

VALENÇAY

Financiers, Farmers General, John Law and Talleyrand were the successive owners; this remarkable castle was very lucky. The colossal and yet elegant keep at the entrance and the roofs and domed towers strike a happy medium between the Renaissance and classical styles. The three courtyards and the apartments are very large. One visits only part of the latter.

It is well-known that Napoleon had Talleyrand purchase Valençay so that he could entertain statesmen here. The most illustrious was King Ferdinand VII of Spain, who was courteously treated while he was a prisoner here from 1808 to 1814.

The former Bishop of Autun lavished care on this residence, which was worthy of his family.

He embellished the castle and added about 20,000 hectares (50,000 acres) to it.

From this period there still remain drawing rooms and handsome furniture which were used for receptions, some of which were magnificent. The Prince's chamber has been reconstituted and historical souvenirs enable us to evoke this relatively faithful servant of many different regimes. In the gardens and on the balustrades magnificently plumed peacocks parade among other birds and animals of various sorts: Valençay is highly colored in every detail.

VILLANDRY

A very beautiful French-style garden "embroidered" with box-trees and yews, where the borders represent the different forms of love, captures our attention so thoroughly that we almost forget the kitchen garden and the water garden with its beautiful mirror-like sheet of water.

This masterpiece, the only one of its kind in France, is due to Dr. Carvallo who, around 1906, decided to reconstruct the former sixteenth-century gardens, which had been created by Gaillon. The owner had to plow up the English garden, clear the moat, reconstruct the terraces and reconnect the circuits of water pipes. Considering the extent and complexity of the work, this was admirably done.

The water, plant geometry and sculpted stone have benefitted more from it than nature, no doubt.

The château is less deserving of admiration because it has been remodelled several times.

Villandry houses a museum of considerable interest (Goya, Herrera, Zurbaran and others).

Jean Le Breton, in the sixteenth century, and, more recently, the Castellanes and even Napoleon and his brother Joseph lived here.

Table of contents

Loire Valley

Photographs

Chateaux of the Loire
is a production
of Editions SUN
Paris, France

Publishers:
Marcel Renébon
Nicolas Imbert
Nicole Imbert

Originator
and artistic director:
Roger Krause

Technical director:
Roger Bougault

Layout director:
Michel Labarthe

Photo-engravers:
Bussière A. G. / Offset 94
S.N.O. / Illustration

Photo-composer:
A.P.S.

Printer:
Firmin-Didot,
Imprimerie Moderne
du Lion

Art paper
by Papeteries Pronoia

Bookbinder:
S.I.R.C.

In the same series:

Vivre en France
by Gaston Bonheur

Vivre à Paris
by Antoine Blondin

A Vilo exclusive

Printing completed
October 30, 1980
**for Editions SUN
Paris, France**